CITY OF

2000

A Climber's Guide

By Dave Bingham

Thanks to my wife Amy for her enduring
support, and to Brad Schilling for his invaluable
expertise. To all my old partners and friends,
thanks for being part of the adventure.

Self-published by Dave Bingham
Copyright by Dave Bingham 2000

Correspondence and new route information
is greatly appreciated.
P.O. Box 1804 Hailey, ID 83333
dbingham@micron.net

Cover: Tony Yaniro on first ascent
of Technicolor (12b)
Cover design by Dave Wheelock - The Image Shop
wheels@sunvalley.net

INTRODUCTION

Welcome to the City of Rocks. This year 2000 edition is my sixth version since 1985, keeping pace with the ever-changing situation at City of Rocks. Currently, access to several prime climbing spots is in transition. The status of the Twin Sisters is still in litigation, with the Access Fund fighting against the unjust closure of these great crags. Elephant Rock and nearby crags have changed ownership for the better, and the opening of the fantastic Castle Rocks (the large group of rock formations just west of Almo) is imminent. Thanks goes out to the Conservation Fund and the Access Fund for having the insight to protect this unique area.

All the historically significant roadside crags (Treasure Rock, Camp Rock, Chicken Rock, etc) below the Twin Sisters junction are officially closed, and the City's premiere hard crag, The Dolphin, is more private than ever. Day to day operations of the Reserve have passed from the faceless bureaucracy of the National Park Service to the more levelheaded stewardship of the Idaho Department of Parks.

Miles of new trails have been built throughout the Circle Creek basin, accessing dozens of unexplored crags and providing great alternatives for non-climbing activities. The new camping reservation system has simplified finding a site - if you plan ahead. Unfortunately, plans for a huge new RV campground just outside the Reserve boundaries continue to move forward, encouraging a new, full-hook-up RV crowd, heavier vehicle use, and possible abuse of the area.

A couple dozen new climbs have sprung up under the Reserve's permit system, including many moderates that have become some of the most popular routes in the City. Climbing ranger Brad Shilling has performed the invaluable service of replacing many old, untrustworthy anchors and bolts. We can all thank Brad and Reserve Superintendent Ned Jackson for their progressive and positive actions.

When the dust settles on access issues in the next couple years, I plan on publishing an all-new, photo-format guide. For now, this book is still the best place to go for the most up-to-date, complete and accurate information on new climbs, new trails, camping and access concerns. Much has changed in the 22 years since I first climbed here, but the City is still as beautiful as ever and it's still a really fun place to climb.

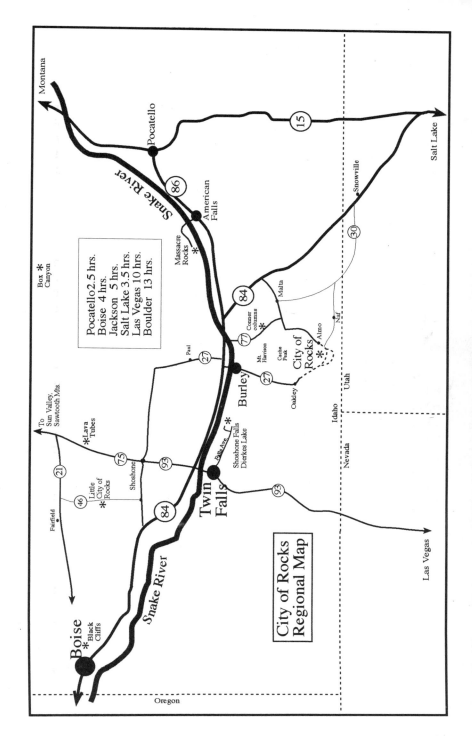

City of Rocks
Regional Map

Pocatello 2.5 hrs.
Boise 4 hrs.
Jackson 5 hrs.
Salt Lake 3.5 hrs.
Las Vegas 10 hrs.
Boulder 13 hrs.

3

AVOIDING DEATH

In recent years there have been numerous accidents involving climbers being dropped while lowering off bolt anchors. Please remember that safety is each individual's responsibility and there is really no excuse for dropping your partner off the end of a rope. Chain anchors are no guarantee that a climb can be done with a single rope. Many popular routes require two ropes (or a bit of careful down climbing at the end). When in doubt, the belayer should tie in or tie a knot in the end of the rope.

This guide makes no attempt to mark routes where an accident could occur (just assume that danger is always lurking) but I will list several popular routes where lowering accidents have happened. These include, but are not limited to:
Fall Line and **Strategic Defense** on Morning Glory Spire.
Just Say No on Elephant Rock.
Redtail on Rabbit Rock.
She's the Bosch on Window Rock.
Provo Wall (most of the bolted routes require two ropes).

The other common cause of accidents are long falls resulting when poorly placed crack protection fails. Many popular moderate routes are surprisingly dangerous because solid protection is difficult or impossible to place. When in doubt, back it up. Better yet, hike around and set up a toprope.
Also, the numbers of bolts shown on topos is a general guide and NOT intended to be an exact bolt count. Please make your own count on site and always carry extra quickdraws for safety.

CLOSED AREAS

The City of Rocks has several access problems including private property, California Trail corridor closures, the Twin Sisters closure, and the Research Natural Area. Thankfully, most of the climbing at the City is fully open public land.

The factor with the most impact on climbers is private land. Several attractive and traditionally used crags are private, and individual owners can decide to allow or disallow climbing on their property. Several landowners at the City are permissive about climbers using their land, while others are not. Most of the landowners are ranchers and are naturally concerned about their cattle being disturbed and fences being damaged. If you do climb on non-posted private land, it is critical to keep a very low profile and avoid areas where animals are grazing .

The southern end of Elephant Rock is still private, although the property has recently changed hands. Efforts are being made to negotiate climber access to both Elephant Rock and the crags to the south, the Gallstone and Checkered Demon. Electric Avenue and the Dungeon are also private, but the owner permits climbing at this time. The Dolphin is very much private, (as it has been all along). Trespassing on any posted area is a bad idea that can jeopardize future relations and impact climber access.

All of the rock formations along the historic California Trail Corridor are officially and permanently closed to climbing. Even though cattle probably do far more damage to historic inscriptions than climbers do, we need to respect the closure. This closure affects City Limits, Chicken Rock, Camp Rock, Elephant Head, Treasure Rock, Saddle Rock, Register Rock as well as miscellaneous minor formations.

A federally designated Research Natural Area (RNA) is located in the north-east edge of the Reserve, north east of Stripe Rock. This is supposed to be a no-use area, closed to hiking as well as climbing. No maps are readily available that show the boundaries of the RNA, so it's difficult to know where you're not supposed to be. Although there are many rock formations, there has been little, if any, recorded climbing in the RNA.

Finally, the Twin Sisters closure is still in litigation as of spring 2000. The NSP conducted a lengthy study of the area to determine negative impacts of climbing on historical elements. They found that climbing was not a significant impact, but closed the area anyway. Hopefully, this unjustified closure will be rescinded in the near future.

CONTENTS

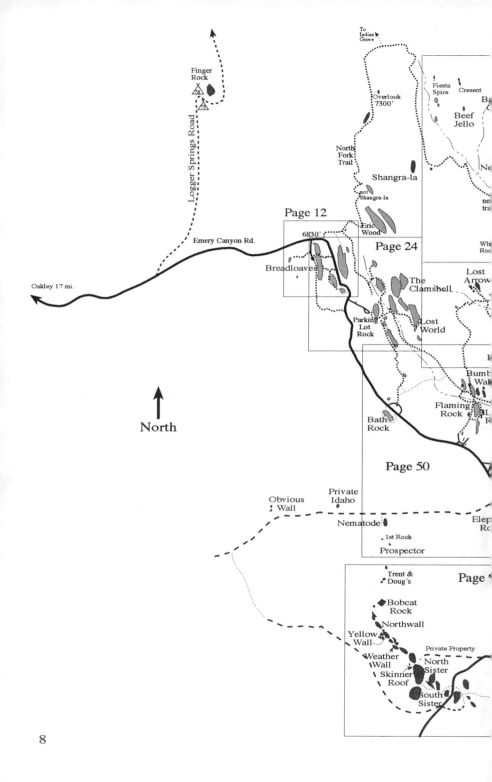

To Indian Grove

Finger Rock

Logger Springs Road

Overlook 7300'

Fiesta Spire

Cresent

Beef Jello

North Fork Trail

Shangra-la

not Shangra-la

Eric Wood

Page 12

6830'

Breadloaves

Emery Canyon Rd.

Oakley 17 mi.

Page 24

Whi Roc

The Clamshell

Lost Arrow

Parking Lot Rock

Lost World

North

Bath Rock

Bumb Wal

Flaming Rock

L R

Page 50

Obvious Wall

Private Idaho

Elep Ro

Nematode

1st Rock

Prospector

Trent & Doug's

Page

Bobcat Rock

Northwall

Yellow Wall

Weather Wall

Skinner Roof

Private Property

North Sister

South Sister

8

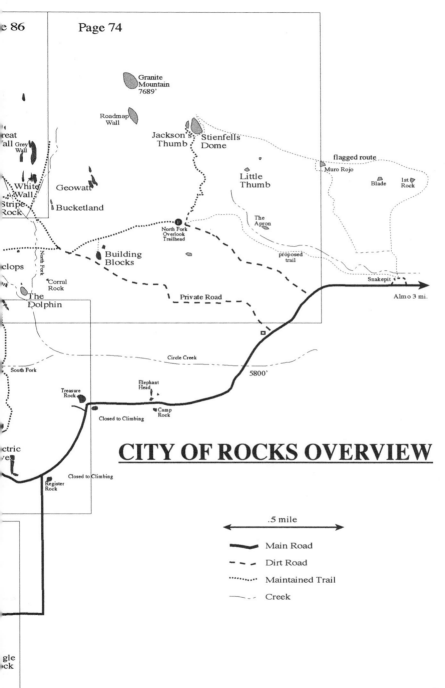

Granite
Mountain
7689'

Roadmap
Wall

reat
all Grey
Wall

Jackson's
Thumb

Stienfells
Dome

flagged route

Muro Rojo

White
Wall

Geowatt

Little
Thumb

Blade

1st
Rock

Stripe
Rock

Bucketland

The
Apron

North Fork
Overlook
Trailhead

clops

North Fork

Building
Blocks

proposed
trail

Corral
Rock

Snakepit

The
Dolphin

Private Road

Almo 3 mi.

South Fork

Circle Creek

5800'

Treasure
Rock

Elephant
Head

Camp
Rock

ctric
ye

Closed to Climbing

CITY OF ROCKS OVERVIEW

Closed to Climbing

Register
Rock

.5 mile

━━━ Main Road

- - - Dirt Road

··········· Maintained Trail

———·— Creek

gle
ck

UPPER CITY

The Upper City, as described here, includes the higher elevation rock formations in the north end of the Reserve. (see map) Included are topos of the Upper and Lower **Breadloaves**, the popular **Decadent Wall**, **Super Hits**, **Owl Rock** and **King on the Throne**.In addition to the routes shown in the topos, check out the following list of less-visited crags.

GO WEST This is the formation just west of the Upper Breadloaves. It is a good spot to go with a group to avoid the often crowded Decadent Wall. The following routes are on the north and west end of the rock, from left to right.
Nature Walk 5.8 TR Look for a single chain anchor.
Strolling 5.8 Climb a face past a tricky start to a single anchor.
Backpacking 5.10 R One bolt, high up, sort of protects this.
Make it Hurt 10a* A nice thin crack on the west end.
Make it Hurt More 11a* The right hand variation. A classic thin crack.
Sunshowers 10 A crack climb somewhere to the right.

UPPER BREADLOAVES - NORTH END
Possible peregrine nesting site. Please don't climb if birds are present.
Route 66 - 5.8 The narrow open book left of the main chimney.
Stolen Thunder 12c* An old Stan Caldwell test piece featuring an ultra-barndoor layback to an offwidth.
Interceptor 11a** The classic overhanging splitter crack. Finger to fist size.
Tide Country 10b* Start as for Interceptor, but stay right.
Descent Route 5.3 Scramble around blocks right of Tide Country.

FINGER ROCK This small tower is located about a half mile up Logger Springs Road, the dirt grade that starts by the Reserve's northeast entrance, on the Oakley road. There are a couple cool campsites here and some worthwhile, out-of-the-way climbs.
Salty Dog 5.9? The obvious splitter offwidth on the west side.
Outland 10a* A slightly dicey, fun face on the south facing prow. Two bolts, one piton.
Toprope 10a* On the east side is a patch of perfect rock. Start in flake, move right. No fixed anchor.
Toprope 10b* Start just right of the flake.

THE MALL Opposite the Upper Breadloaves is the dome-like Shingle Butte. Three climbs can be found in a sheltered alcove on the northeast side, from right to left.

Dragonfly 5.9 A very short, obvious crack on the right end of the wall. Bushes.

The Color of Money 11* Look for bolts protecting the smooth lower face.

Nine to Five Flake 10 An old-school route with marginal protection in hollow flakes. Finishes in a large corner.

ERIC WOOD a.k.a. **TOP ROCK, THE CAMEL** These are the obvious large crags that can be seen to the east of the Upper Breadloaves. With the new Circle Creek Loop trail passing by the base, this area is ripe for new routes. Climbs have been done, but information is sketchy. Check it out!

SHANGRA-LA An out-of-the-way crag with some really cool routes and a hilly 30-minute approach. Start on the trail across from the water pump. (see overview map on page 8). From the saddle just north of the highest rocks, hike down (east, about 450 vertical feet below) to the west face of the formation. Look for the big "window" on the upper right face. Ignore the rock near the saddle that is mis-marked Shangra-La in Calderone's guide. From left to right.

Comatoast 11b*. A 10-bolt line on the left end.

Stick Like A Maggot 11d*. 8 bolts

Beyond Good And Evil 10d** A pretty obvious gear-pro. crack line.

Land Of The Lost 12a. A 10 bolt line on the right.

UPPER CITY -
BREADLOAVES / DECADENT WALL

West

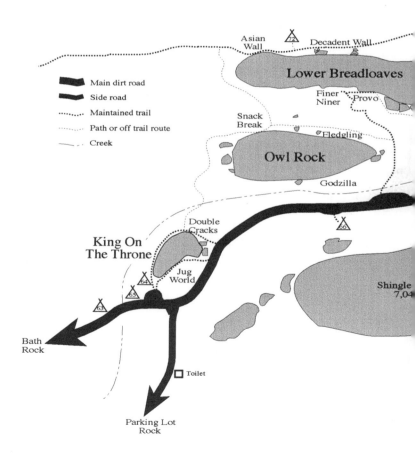

▰▰▰	Main dirt road
▬▬	Side road
·········	Maintained trail
··········	Path or off trail route
— · · —	Creek

Asian Wall

Decadent Wall

Lower Breadloaves

Finer Niner   Provo

Snack Break

Fledgling

Owl Rock

Godzilla

Double Cracks

King On The Throne

Jug World

Shingle 7,04

Bath Rock

☐ Toilet

Parking Lot Rock

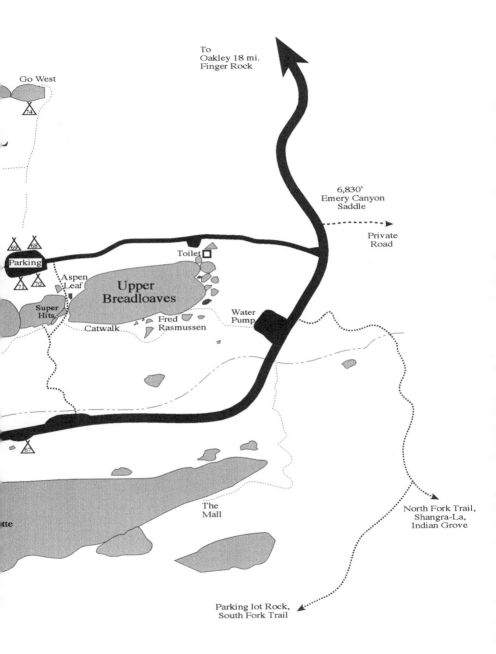

Go West

To
Oakley 18 mi.
Finger Rock

6,830'
Emery Canyon
Saddle

Private
Road

Parking

Toilet

Aspen
Leaf

Upper
Breadloaves

Super
Hits

Catwalk

Fred
Rasmussen

Water
Pump

The
Mall

North Fork Trail,
Shangra-La,
Indian Grove

Parking lot Rock,
South Fork Trail

UPPER BREADLOAVES—EAST

A NO CASH REFUNDS 7
B LOST PIONEERS 9d*
C URBAN RENEWALL 11a*
   (R.P.'s)
D BAD MANNERS 11b*
E FRED RASMUSSEN 8*
F X 10
G GROOVE BOOK 8
H ENGLISH MUFFIN 9
I MANKY SCUM 7

J THE EGYPTIAN 8*
K DESCENT ROUTE 5
L CATWALK 8*
M REID'S ROUTE 9
N ROMAN MEAL 8
O BURGER CLING 9

UPPER BREADLOAVES—WEST

A WIDE CRACKS 8
B UNKNOWN 12?
C ASPEN LEAF 9*
D SLANDER AT CONNER CR. 12 TR
E TELAVIV 12b**
F STREACHMARKS 9*
G BARN DOOR 11 (20ft. crack)

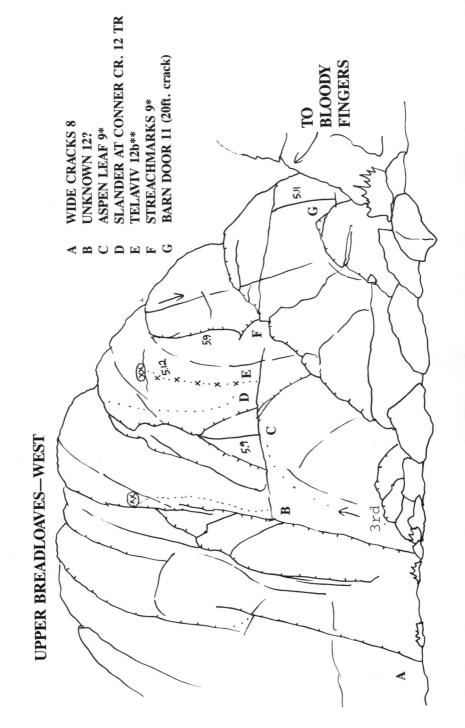

TO BLOODY FINGERS

DECADENT WALL

Authors note: Several "offensive" route names in this area have been modified or deleted.

A   6
B   WATERSPORTS 6
C   SUBMISSION 6
D   CAROL'S CRACK 8**
E   FLESH FOR FANTASY 11a*
F   DIVINE DECADENCE 9-
G   ADOLESCENT HOMOSAPIEN 7**
H   10a*
I   BESTIALITY 9

J   7x
K   11a*
L   10a*
M   8*
N   10c**
O   LIFE WITHOUT SEX 11
P   ESTROGEN IMBALANCE 10c/d*
Q   SEXUAL DYSFUNCTION 12a
R   FRIGIDITY 12a*
S   TESTOSTERONE TEST 11d**
    (#0 tcu. friends)
T   IMPOTENCE 10d*
U   SEX,DRUGS, ROCK& ROLL 11a*

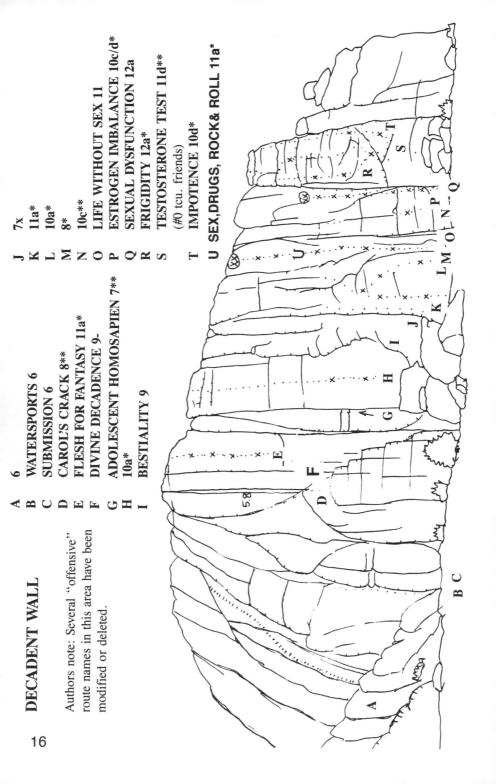

ASIAN WALL—LOWER DECADENT

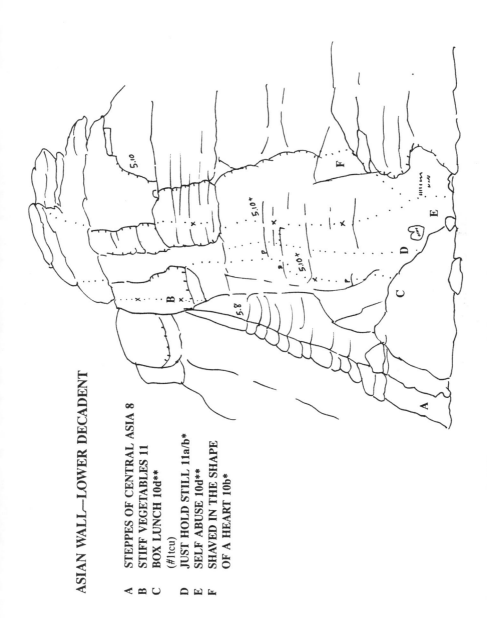

A   **STEPPES OF CENTRAL ASIA 8**
B   **STIFF VEGETABLES 11**
C   **BOX LUNCH 10d****
       (#1tcu)
D   **JUST HOLD STILL 11a/b***
E   **SELF ABUSE 10d****
F   **SHAVED IN THE SHAPE**
       OF A HEART 10b*

SUPER HITS WALL—BLOODY FINGERS

A HOSTAGE DRAMA 9
B DOUBLE VISION 10a*
C OCTOBER 8
D YELLOW PAGES 8TR
E BLOODY FINGERS 10a***
F NEW TOY 10b*
G CHIMNEY 6

H TWIST & CRAWL 8*
I MYSTERY ACHIEVEMENT 7r
J INTRUDING DIKE 7**
K HOUGH'S CRACK 7
L JOHN WAYNE NEVER WORE LYCRA 11b
M BARYSNOKOV NEVER
   WORE CAMO 12TR

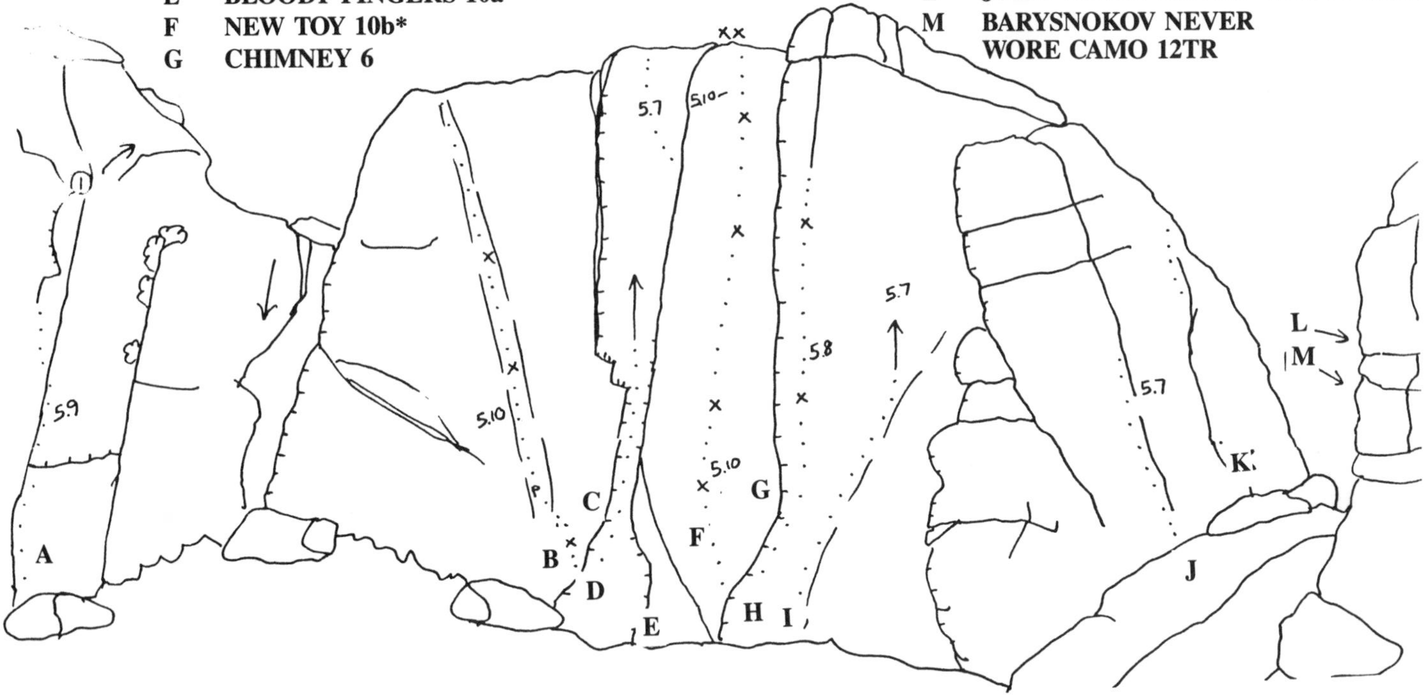

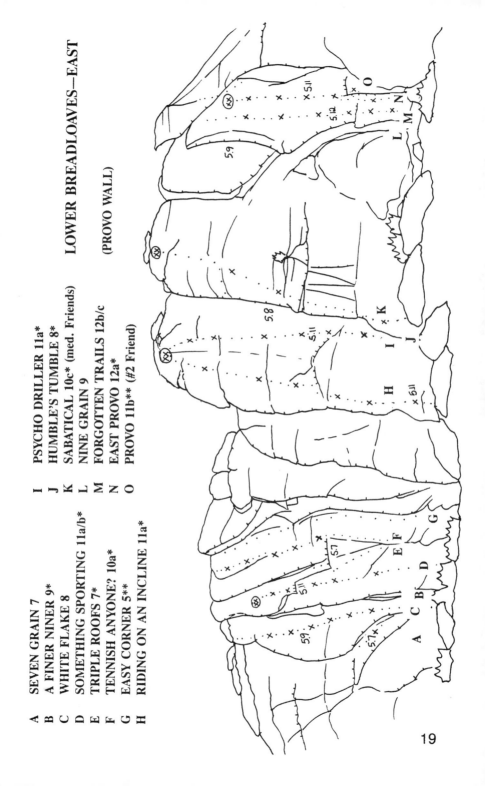

LOWER BREADLOAVES—EAST

(PROVO WALL)

A SEVEN GRAIN 7
B A FINER NINER 9*
C WHITE FLAKE 8
D SOMETHING SPORTING 11a/b*
E TRIPLE ROOFS 7*
F TENNISH ANYONE? 10a*
G EASY CORNER 5**
H RIDING ON AN INCLINE 11a*

I PSYCHO DRILLER 11a*
J HUMBLE'S TUMBLE 8*
K SABATICAL 10c* (med. Friends)
L NINE GRAIN 9
M FORGOTTEN TRAILS 12b/c
N EAST PROVO 12a*
O PROVO 11b** (#2 Friend)

19

OWL ROCK

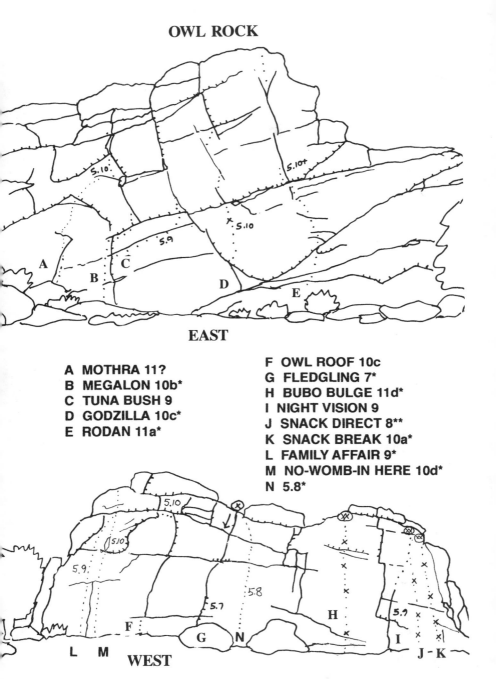

EAST

A MOTHRA 11?
B MEGALON 10b*
C TUNA BUSH 9
D GODZILLA 10c*
E RODAN 11a*

F OWL ROOF 10c
G FLEDGLING 7*
H BUBO BULGE 11d*
I NIGHT VISION 9
J SNACK DIRECT 8**
K SNACK BREAK 10a*
L FAMILY AFFAIR 9*
M NO-WOMB-IN HERE 10d*
N 5.8*

WEST

Note: To avoid disturbing nesting owls, please avoid "Owl Roof" until late summer.

KING ON THE THRONE

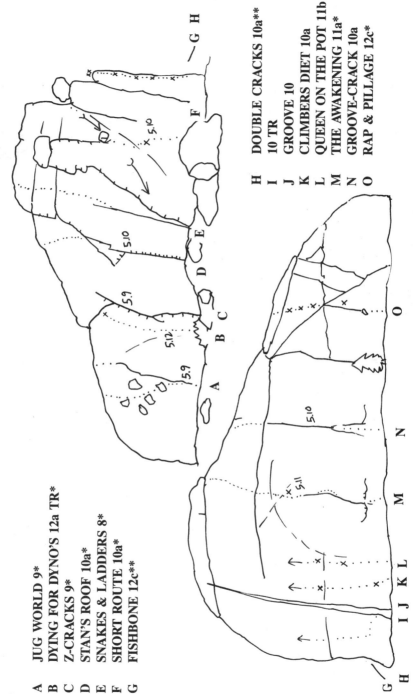

A   JUG WORLD 9*
B   DYING FOR DYNO'S 12a TR*
C   Z-CRACKS 9*
D   STAN'S ROOF 10a*
E   SNAKES & LADDERS 8*
F   SHORT ROUTE 10a*
G   FISHBONE 12c**

H   DOUBLE CRACKS 10a**
I   10 TR
J   GROOVE 10
K   CLIMBERS DIET 10a
L   QUEEN ON THE POT 11b
M   THE AWAKENING 11a*
N   GROOVE-CRACK 10a
O   RAP & PILLAGE 12c*

PARKING LOT ROCK AREA

The Parking Lot Rock area is probably the most heavily used area at the City. The best crags are clustered in a tight group where you will find quick access to dozens of high quality climbs of all difficulties. Let's do our best to try and minimize our impact on this unique place.

On a practical note, it's helpful to know that many of the rock formations at the City are long, fin shaped features that run in a north-south direction, with the main walls facing east or west. Seek the shade or sun accordingly.

Expect popular routes like Delay of Game, Scream Cheese, Skyline, etc. to be crowded at times. When climbing these City classics, please be considerate of others by not monopolizing routes with topropes and large groups. Remember, there are many great routes that are often overlooked because they are slightly less obvious than the chalk-plastered trade routes.

In addition to the climbs shown in topo format, the following is a list of several other worthy crags for your climbing pleasure.

HANGDOG DOME This is the sizable formation that sits up on the hill behind Animal Cracker Dome. A few gear routes have been done on the right side, but the steeper left side has room for good-looking bolted routes.

BAD BOY A small crag just east of "The Office".
Bad Boy 11aR One bolt doesn't make the ground any softer.
Rubble without a Pause 10R The name says it all. The flake to the right of Bad Boy.

PETER PAN BOULDER Just west of Lower Creekside Tower is a little boulder with three grungy but groovy top-rope problems. Very steep! From left to right.
Peter Pan 11* Captain Hook 11* Wendy 11*

THE CLOSET The shady corridor on the extreme south end of Creekside Tower. Two micro-classics lurk at the far left end.
Aggro Betty 11b** The left route. Steep.
Going Down to Almo with a Lipstick in My Purse 11c** Originally rated 14a, a must for aspiring big wall climbers. The right route.

RABBIT TAIL As the name suggests, this is the southern "tail" of Rabbit Rock. All the climbs listed are located on the east side of the rock, and are accessed by the trail that connects the Redtail area of Rabbit Rock with The Drilling Fields. Bring cams and nuts. From left to right.

Permutation 12b** A bolt protected crack line.

Variable 11c* Just right of, and sharing anchors withPermutation.

Separation Anxiety 11a* Pass a bolt near the bottom to mixed climbing and moss above.

Response To Grace 11b* A steep start to a face that passes left of a prominent diagonal crack.

Drill Or Be Killed 10d* Five bolts and gear crosses the diagonal crack up high.

Geologic Warfare 11c/d* Crack climb a diagonal crack feature to a crux face finish with bolts and anchor.

Right To The Point 11d* Start on dicey friction with bolt protection.

Running On Empty 11b* Just right of previous route. Bolts, friction and gear.

BLOCKHEAD Just south of Buzzard Perch, and east of Rabbit Rock, this formation has a prominent fractured block.

Blockhead 10a Climb a slab through a tree to gain the obvious splitter hand crack just right of the block.

The Crack in the corner is rumored to be about 5.9

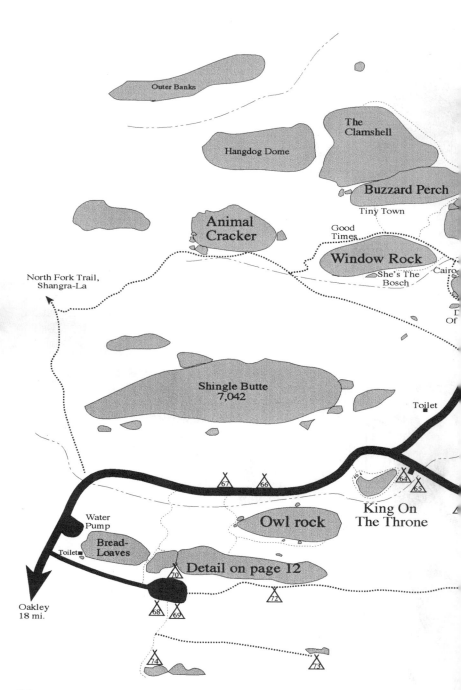

Outer Banks

The Clamshell

Hangdog Dome

Buzzard Perch

Tiny Town

Animal Cracker

Good Times

Window Rock

She's The Bosch

Cairo

North Fork Trail, Shangra-La

Shingle Butte
7,042

Toilet

67
66
79
64
65

King On The Throne

Water Pump

Owl rock

Bread-Loaves

Toilet

70

Detail on page 12

72

Oakley
18 mi.

68
69

74
73

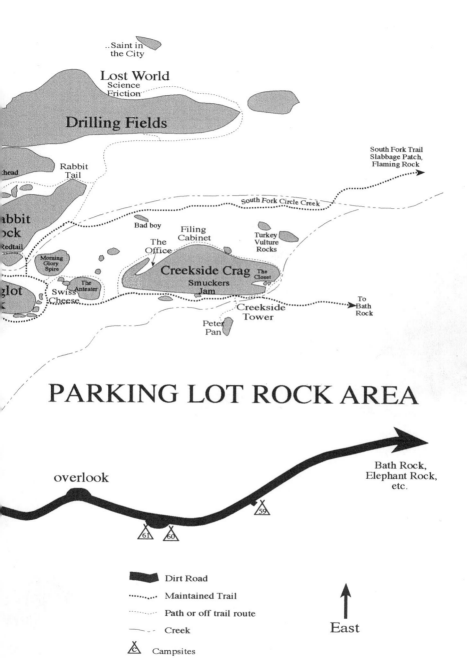

..Saint in
the City

Lost World
Science
Friction

Drilling Fields

Rabbit
Tail

South Fork Trail
Slabbage Patch,
Flaming Rock

..head

abbit
ock

Redtail

South Fork Circle Creek

Bad boy

Filing
Cabinet

Turkey
Vulture
Rocks

The
Office

Morning
Glory
Spire

glot

Creekside Crag

The
Closet

The
Anteater

Smuckers
Jam

Swiss
Cheese

To
Bath
Rock

Creekside
Tower

Peter
Pan

PARKING LOT ROCK AREA

overlook

Bath Rock,
Elephant Rock,
etc.

59

61   60

	Dirt Road
..........-	Maintained Trail
....	Path or off trail route
— - -	Creek
⚠	Campsites

East

25

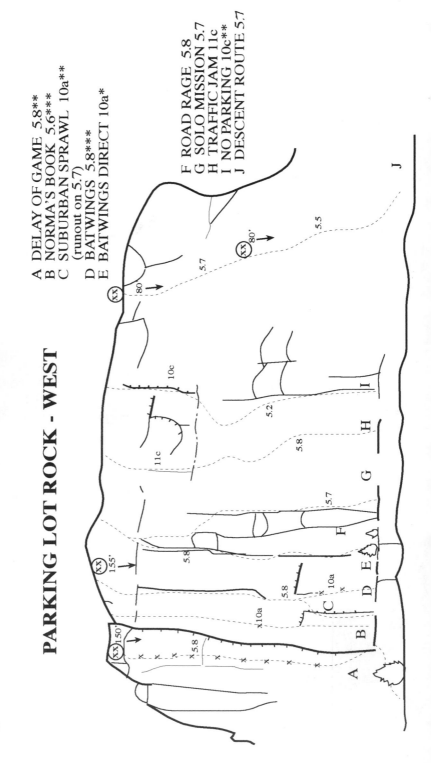

PARKING LOT ROCK - WEST

A DELAY OF GAME 5.8**
B NORMA'S BOOK 5.6***
C SUBURBAN SPRAWL 10a**
  (runout on 5.7)
D BATWINGS 5.8***
E BATWINGS DIRECT 10a*

F ROAD RAGE 5.8
G SOLO MISSION 5.7
H TRAFFIC JAM 11c
I NO PARKING 10c**
J DESCENT ROUTE 5.7

26

PARKING LOT ROCK - EAST SIDE

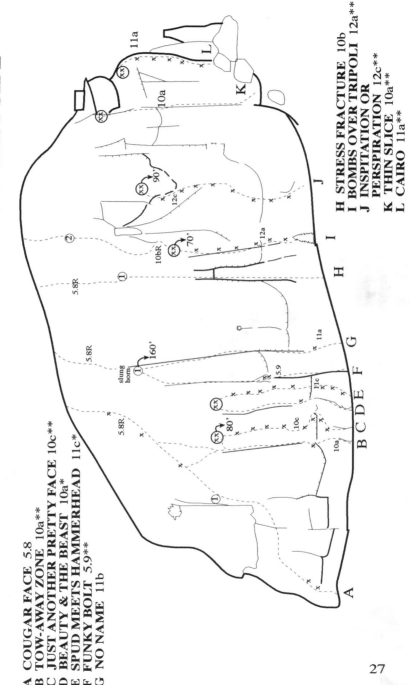

A COUGAR FACE 5.8
B TOW-AWAY ZONE 10a**
C JUST ANOTHER PRETTY FACE 10c**
D BEAUTY & THE BEAST 10a*
E SPUD MEETS HAMMERHEAD 11c*
F FUNKY BOLT 5.9**
G NO NAME 11b

H STRESS FRACTURE 10b
I BOMBS OVER TRIPOLI 12a**
J INSPITATION OR
   PERSPIRATION 12c**
K THIN SLICE 10a**
L CAIRO 11a**

27

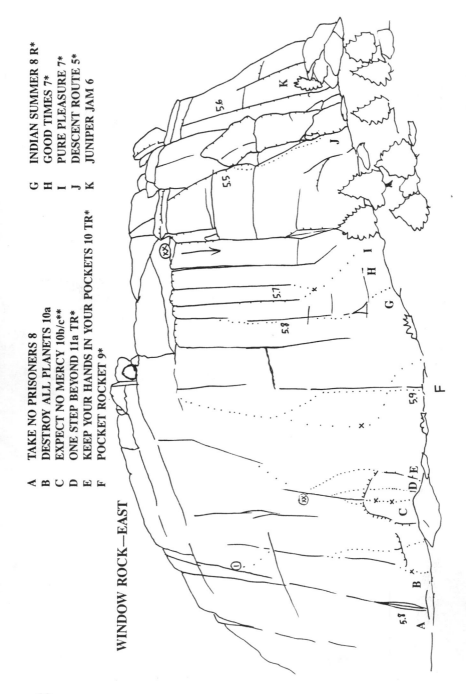

WINDOW ROCK—EAST

A TAKE NO PRISONERS 8
B DESTROY ALL PLANETS 10a
C EXPECT NO MERCY 10b/c**
D ONE STEP BEYOND 11a TR*
E KEEP YOUR HANDS IN YOUR POCKETS 10 TR*
F POCKET ROCKET 9*

G INDIAN SUMMER 8 R*
H GOOD TIMES 7*
I PURE PLEASURE 7*
J DESCENT ROUTE 5*
K JUNIPER JAM 6

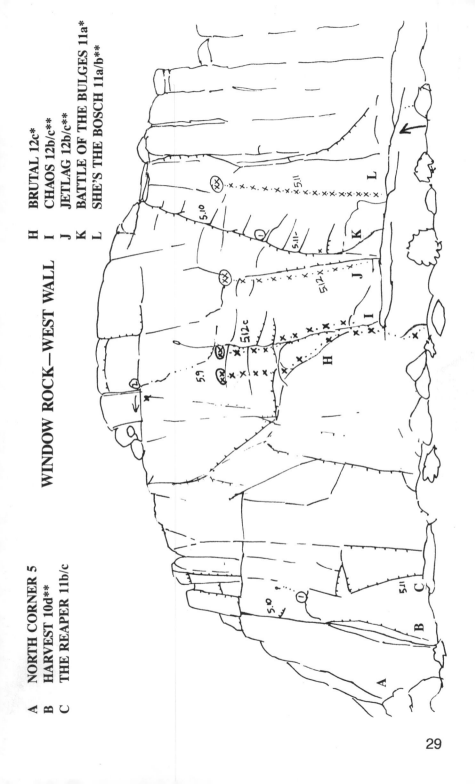

WINDOW ROCK—WEST WALL

A NORTH CORNER 5
B HARVEST 10d**
C THE REAPER 11b/c

H BRUTAL 12c*
I CHAOS 12b/c**
J JETLAG 12b/c**
K BATTLE OF THE BULGES 11a*
L SHE'S THE BOSCH 11a/b**

29

ANIMAL CRACKER DOME

A   A MAN SHOULD NEVER GAMBLE 6

B   THE ASSASSIN 10a
     (thin cr./pin, move r.
       around corner)

C   GRIEVOUS BODILY HARM 8r

D   ODE TO A DEAD RANGER 11c/d

E   ANIMAL CRACKER 10a**

BUZZARD PERCH

A   **BODY GOD 11a***
B   **WAFER OF WOE 11a**
C   **DOGGIE BOD 11?**
D   **FAT LIP 12a****
E   **TERROR OF TINY TOWN 11a*****
       (tcu's to 2')
F   **GHETTO BLASTER 12**

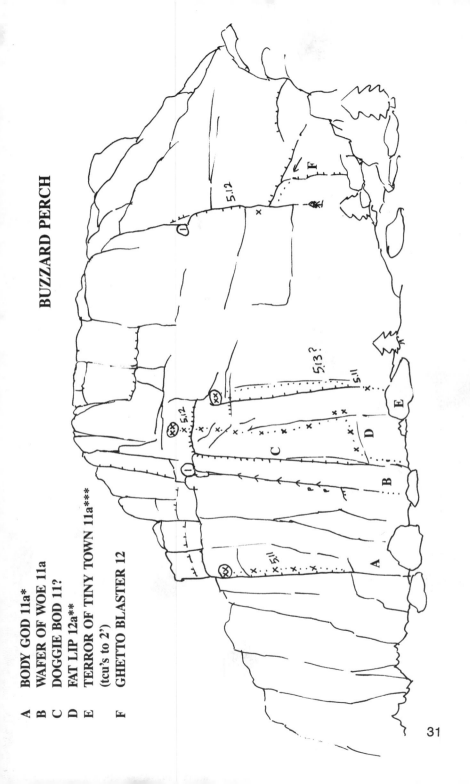

RABBIT ROCK—NORTHEAST FACE

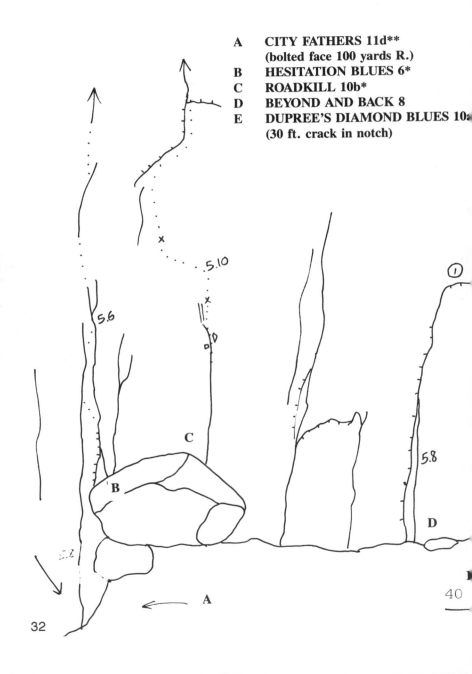

A	**CITY FATHERS 11d****
	(bolted face 100 yards R.)
B	**HESITATION BLUES 6***
C	**ROADKILL 10b***
D	**BEYOND AND BACK 8**
E	**DUPREE'S DIAMOND BLUES 10:**
	(30 ft. crack in notch)

5.10

5.6

5.8

①

C

B

D

A

RABBIT ROCK—WEST FACE

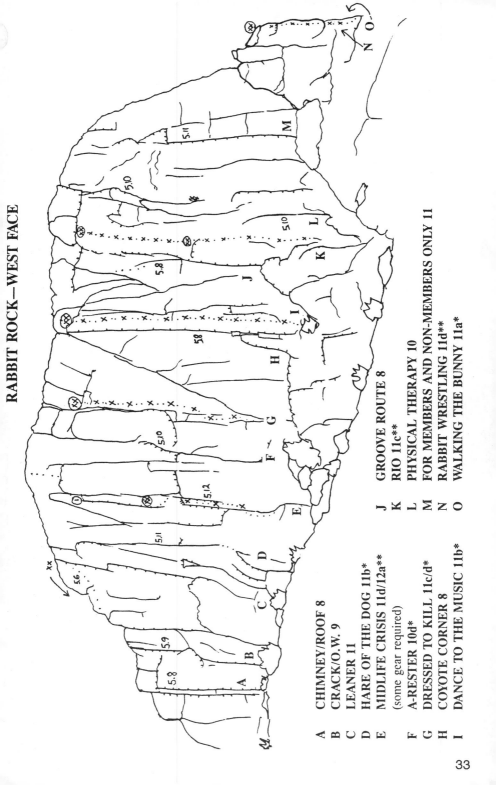

A   CHIMNEY/ROOF 8
B   CRACK/O.W. 9
C   LEANER 11
D   HARE OF THE DOG 11b*
E   MIDLIFE CRISIS 11d/12a**
    (some gear required)
F   A-RESTER 10d*
G   DRESSED TO KILL 11c/d*
H   COYOTE CORNER 8
I   DANCE TO THE MUSIC 11b*

J   GROOVE ROUTE 8
K   RIO 11c**
L   PHYSICAL THERAPY 10
M   FOR MEMBERS AND NON-MEMBERS ONLY 11
N   RABBIT WRESTLING 11d**
O   WALKING THE BUNNY 11a*

SPUD WALL

RABBIT ROCK

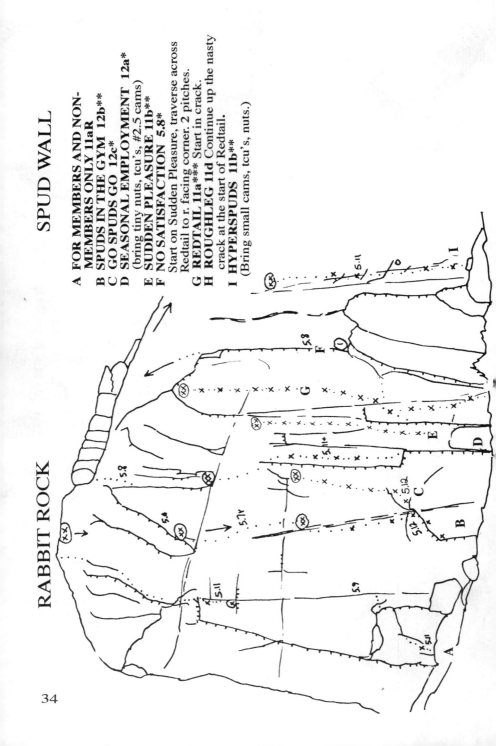

A FOR MEMBERS AND NON-MEMBERS ONLY 11aR

B SPUDS IN THE GYM 12b**

C GO SPUDS GO 12c*

D SEASONAL EMPLOYMENT 12a*
(bring tiny nuts, tcu's, #2.5 cams)

E SUDDEN PLEASURE 11b**

F NO SATISFACTION 5.8*
Start on Sudden Pleasure, traverse across Redtail to r. facing corner. 2 pitches.

G REDTAIL 11a*** Start in crack.

H ROUGHLEG 11d Continue up the nasty crack at the start of Redtail.

I HYPERSPUDS 11b**
(Bring small cams, tcu's, nuts.)

MORNING GLORY SPIRE a.k.a. THE INCISOR

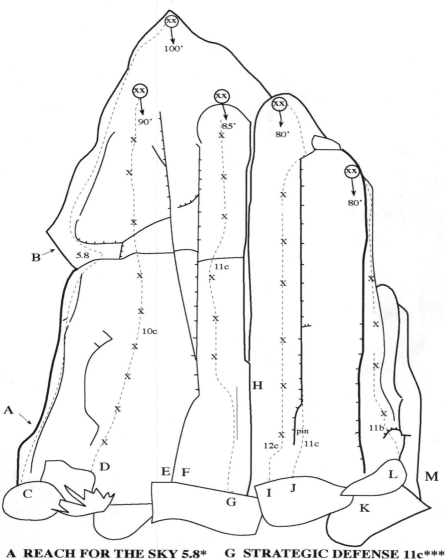

A **REACH FOR THE SKY 5.8***
B **VEAL CAGE 12c***
C **SKYLINE 5.8****
D **FALL LINE 10c****
E **ACCEPTABLE RISK 10d***
F **BROWN FLAKE 10d****

G **STRATEGIC DEFENSE 11c*****
H **INCISOR CHIMNEY 5.8***
I **POWER TOOLS 12c*****
J **CRACK OF DOOM 11c*****
K **BOOK OF DISSENT 10a***
L **SIESTA 11b****
M **DESCENT ROUTE 5.5***

THE ANTEATER—WEST

Descent: Rap
Swiss Cheese.
(1 rope)

A   **SHE-BOP 9**
B   **SWISS CHEESE 7R***
C   **SCREAM CHEESE 9****
D   **HOLDING OUT FOR A HERO 10b R***
E   **WHEAT FAT 11b**
F   **BODY SNATCHER 10d**
G   **SMURF SMASHER 11a**

H   **FLYBOY 10d***
I   **VELVEETA 8TR****

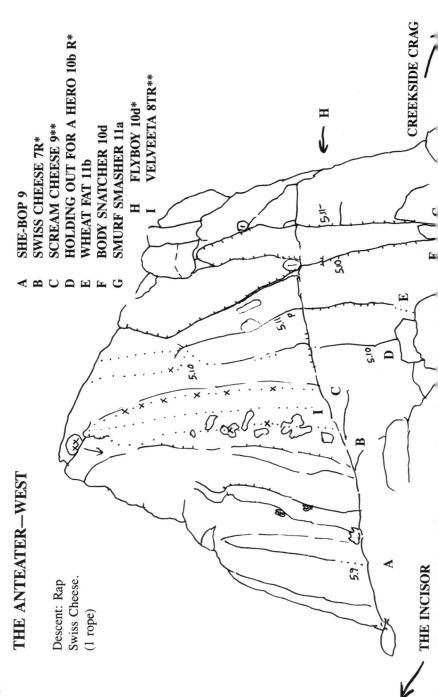

CREEKSIDE CRAG

THE INCISOR

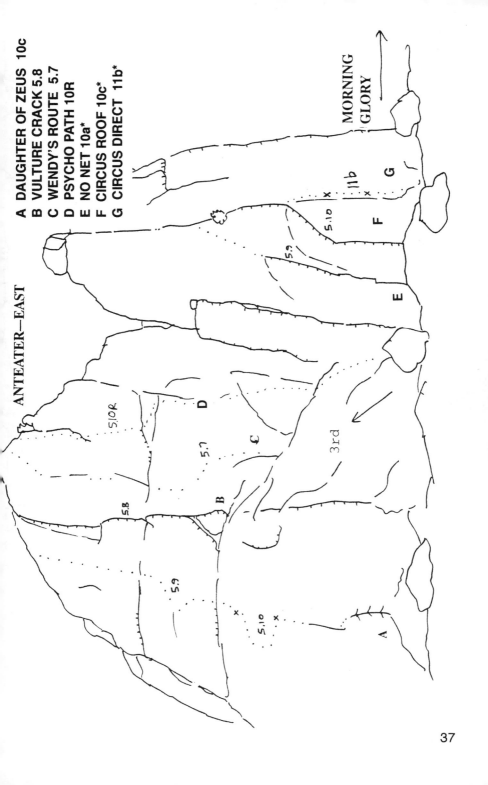

ANTEATER—EAST

A DAUGHTER OF ZEUS 10c
B VULTURE CRACK 5.8
C WENDY'S ROUTE 5.7
D PSYCHO PATH 10R
E NO NET 10a*
F CIRCUS ROOF 10c*
G CIRCUS DIRECT 11b*

MORNING GLORY

37

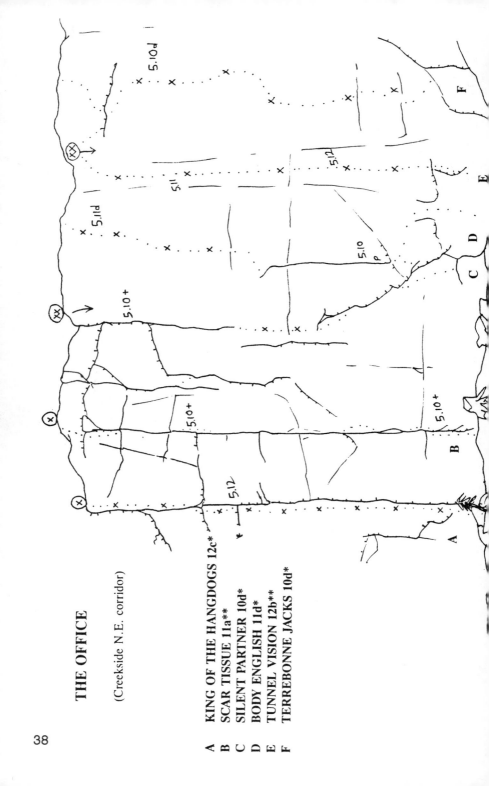

THE OFFICE

(Creekside N.E. corridor)

A   KING OF THE HANGDOGS 12c*
B   SCAR TISSUE 11a**
C   SILENT PARTNER 10d*
D   BODY ENGLISH 11d*
E   TUNNEL VISION 12b**
F   TERREBONNE JACKS 10d*

THE FILING CABINET—(LOWER OFFICE)

These routes require nuts/Friends

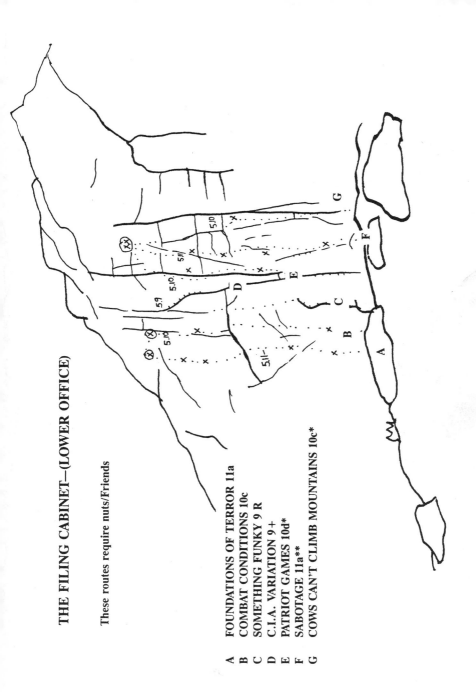

- A FOUNDATIONS OF TERROR 11a
- B COMBAT CONDITIONS 10c
- C SOMETHING FUNKY 9 R
- D C.I.A. VARIATION 9+
- E PATRIOT GAMES 10d*
- F SABOTAGE 11a**
- G COWS CAN'T CLIMB MOUNTAINS 10c*

39

THE DRILLING FIELDS—(LOST WORLD—WEST)

A   LOVE WITHOUT DESIRE 7
B   BILL PICKLE 11b
C   DRILLED PICKLES 12
D   THE DRILLING FIELDS 11b**
E   PIGS ON A WING 11a*

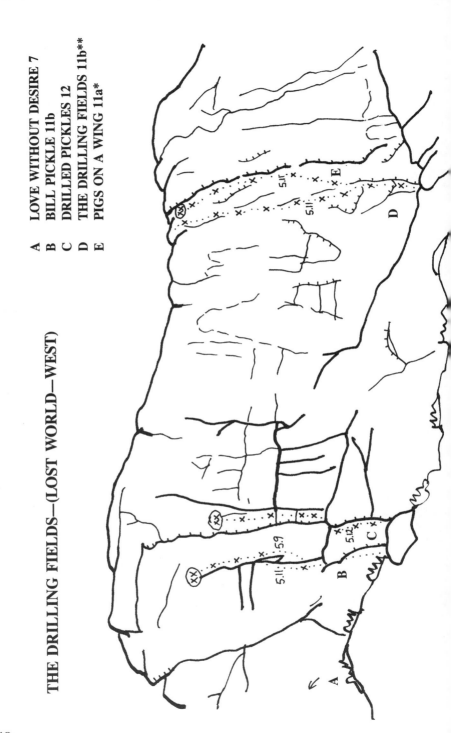

LOST WORLD - (DRILLING FIELDS EAST)

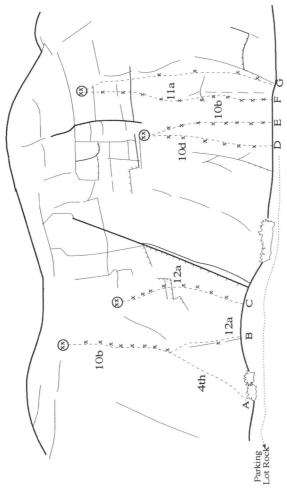

Access by scrambling over the south end of the Drilling Fields formation.

A YANKEE CLIPPER 10b*
B CLIPPER DIRECT 12a
  (One move off the ground)
C GOLDEN CORRAL 12a*

D LOST SOLES 10d*
E TRUTH IS STRANGER
  THAN FRICTION 10b**
F SCIENCE FRICTION 11a**
G OLD UNKNOWN 10R
  IT'S HARD TO BE A SAINT
  IN THE CITY 11c** A 3-bolt
  corner, on rock 250' to the east.

UPPER CREEKSIDE SLABS—WEST

A OLD TIMER 5*
B THIS SPUD'S FOR YOU 10b R
C BIG CITY DORK 10a R

D DOUBLE DRIBBLE 8
E CORNER KICK 7
F STAIRWAY 9*

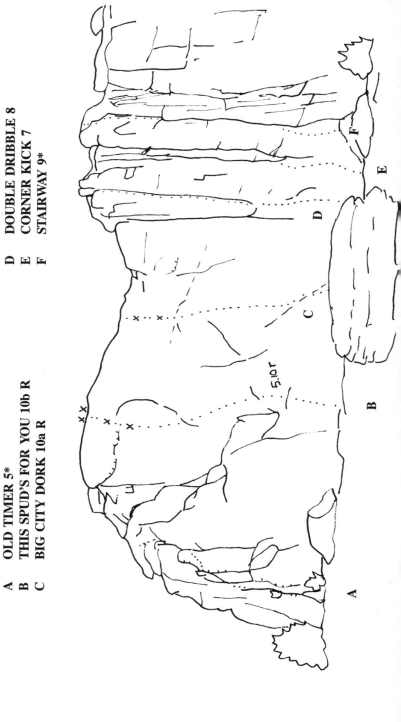

LOWER CREEKSIDE—WEST

A MARK'S CORNER 10d
B LESBIAN KNIFE FIGHT 12b*
C MODERNA ZEITEN 11c/d**
D BOULDER URBANO 11a*
E ELFWORKS 11a*
F SMUCKERS JAM 9
G ALTERED LIFE FORMS 12a/b*
H DIRE STRAIGHTS 9*
I NAIROBI 12a**
J ROID VOID 11b/c
K SNAKE CHARMER 11d*

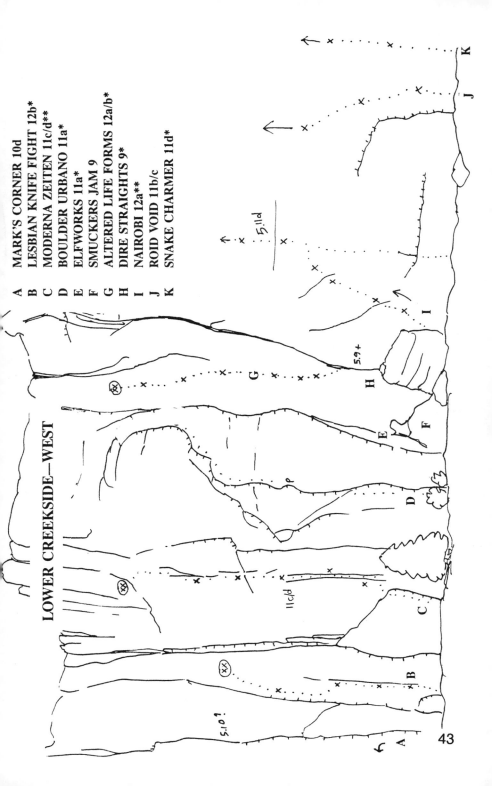

43

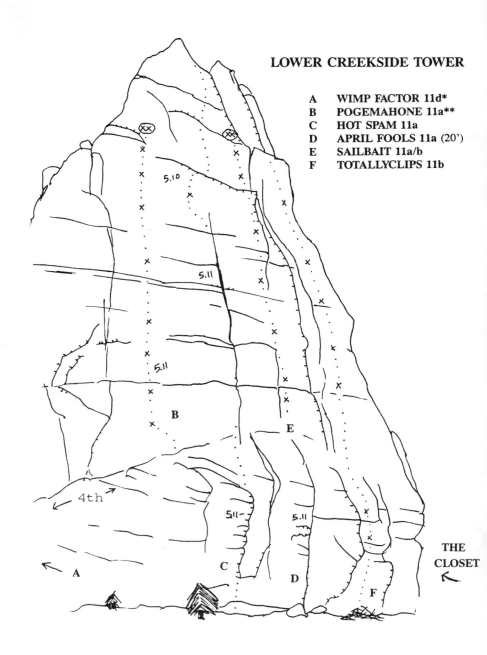

LOWER CREEKSIDE TOWER

A   WIMP FACTOR 11d*
B   POGEMAHONE 11a**
C   HOT SPAM 11a
D   APRIL FOOLS 11a (20')
E   SAILBAIT 11a/b
F   TOTALLYCLIPS 11b

5.10

5.11

5.11

B

E

4th

5.11-

5.11

A

C

D

F

THE
CLOSET

44

NOTES:

CENTER CITY

For lack of a better name, Center City refers to the area south of the Parking Lot Rock area, including roadside crags like **Bath** and **Elephant Rock**. Also in this area are the scenic climbs along South Creek, including **Flaming Rock**, **Transformer Corridor** and **Bumblie Wall**. South Creek is about a half mile walk from camp site #39 on a good trail. Despite the well marked trails, the area is a bit of a maze, and can be confusing for first time visitors. Check the map and have fun exploring.

Much of the land to the south of the main road is private, the notable exception being **Bath Rock**. At the time of this writing, several formations are closed, including the south half of Elephant Rock, **The Gallstone** and **Checkered Demon**. However, access to these crags is currently being negotiated, and may soon change. The **Electric Avenue** area and **The Dungeon** are also privately owned, but are not posted against trespass. If you climb here, take care and use only the main path, which begins by The Dungeon.

Climbs along the historic "California Trail" are now permanently closed. These include **Register Rock, Treasure Rock, Kaiser's Helmet, Camp Rock, Chicken Rock** and **Elephant Head.** Climbs not shown in topos include the following:

THE WART This is the small blob of rock just north of the Bath Rock parking area, behind site #55. Three toprope routes can be found on the east side.
Flake 5.8 Beware of resident bats!
Move with a View 5.9+ The center face.
Right Side 5.9* Start in a crack and finish on crux face moves.

BATH ROCK - SOUTHWEST BUTTRESS
The following routes can be found, right to left, past the bolted corner/ arete, "Prey for Me".
Chimney / Crack 5.6 Climb the left side of the major crack, about 20' left of "Prey".
White Hueco's 5.11a* Look for bolts on a bulge.
Sandbag Route 5.8R* This takes the right side of the prominent alcove about 50' left of "Prey for Me". Despite the name, and R rating, a pretty cool route.
Calamari 5.12a/b** Scramble up (fourth class) to a belay ledge at the base of the steep alcove. Good steep fun.

Rebar Route 3rd class* Probably the most popular and dangerous route on the rock, made more difficult by the addition of the rebar by unknown persons in the early 80's.

Dial 5.8 Hardly worth mentioning. Short crack left of the Rebar Route.

PRIVATE IDAHO Actually on public land and fully open for climbing. This sweet little crag is located on the two-track road, high in the saddle, west of Elephant Rock, a short ways above the Nematode.

White Line Fever 11a** Follow the mysterious white line past several bolts on excellent steep rock.

Crotchbound 11b* (What happens when you hang too long.) Bolts right of "White Line Fever".

FIRST ROCK From the Nematode, walk south to find a small rock with an attractive arete. **First Rock Arete 10d*** with one piton and two bolts.

PROSPECTOR ROCK From the Nematode, walk south for about a quarter mile to find two climbs on the southwest side of a sizable rock.

Mother Lode 12a* Six bolts to chains on steep white rock.

The Shaft 10b* A stemmy route with five bolts and a single point anchor.

THE OBVIOUS WALL Continue on down the two-track past Private Idaho.

Obviously Leftover 10c Four bolts. The left-most route.

Loner With A Boner 10d** Obvious left hand route.

Another Obvious Route 10b/c*

Obviously Pinched 5.8 The right-hand route, finishing in a crack.

Don't Have a Cow Man 5.7 On the rock right of the Obvious Wall. The left-trending crack line.

VITAL SIGNS 11C* An insignificant rock (and route) with a steep right leaning crack. Bouldering? Look for this opposite the road from the Dungeon, out in the meadow a bit.

Colon Cleanser 10d* A short, sweet bolted route located about 100' north of the road junction below Elephant Rock. See map.

CRYSTAL COW Located about 700' east of Practice Rock.
Udder Delight 12a** Five Bolts on excellent rock.
Right Route 11d Three bolts.

BOULDERING AREA The standard bouldering at the City is the group of boulders across from Practice Rock, around the Turtle Rock Cave, and generally in the vicinity of campsites #10 thru #26. The coarse rock tends to be pretty hard on the tips and can be counter-productive to your roped climbing. Nevertheless, City bouldering can be a lot of fun, and several spots have been worked including the Elderberry Boulder (see map) and the rocks south of the Nematode formation. If you are serious about bouldering, check out Dierke's Lake, near Twin Falls, Idaho. (See page 121 for details.)

LOOKOUT ROCK This is the massive formation east of Flaming Rock that can be easily climbed from campsite #29. This route is a classic (fourth class) scramble up the south ridge with a fantastic view of the whole area. Highly recommended. There are a few routes on the west and north faces (listed below) that don't see much traffic.
All Alone in the Big City 10a Start at the toe of the west face, following the middle of three orange streaks and passing a couple small roofs.
Tubed With a View 10c Climb the left hand orange streak, past a bolt. Climb through the "tube" and up a face with two more old bolts. Bring a 4" cam.
Gonzo Dog Brains 5.8 A broken crack line left of the orange streak area.
North Face 5.8 An old route that apparently climbs the broken north end of the formation.

FLAMING ROCK
Baked Beings From Hell 10r On the extreme north end of Flaming Rock's west side, about 30' from the trail, look for a featured vertical start with one bolt leading to runout climbing on a slabby ridge. This nice line could use some more bolts.

RADICELLA ROCK The uninspiring fin to your right as you walk down towards Flaming Rock. There are some good possibilities for beginner routes here.
Micro Pillar 11a (a.k.a. Radicella Face.) A three-bolt route to the right of the trail, on the tail end of the formation.

PUZZLE WALL From the trail on the east side of Flaming Rock, this is the larger patina wall just west of the trail.
Flaven Face 11b* Pass the thin slab to the beautiful patina.

CANNIBAL CORRIDOR Just downstream from the Transformer Corridor, look for the overhanging start of "Get Over It". The following are listed right to left.
Get Over It 11a* A short overhang followed by a moderate face.
Cannibal's Delight 12b* Located about 50' left of Get Over It, an awkward start leads to thin face-climbing.
HACKER ROCK Continue up the corridor and look for these routes on a separate rock about 75' past Cannibal's Delight.
Right 10 Toprope The best looking face, but with a single point anchor and no lead bolts.
Center 5.9 Two bolts plus gear.
Left 10a The two bolts don't help much when you need it.

HUMMINGBIRD CORRIDOR (a.k.a. California Corridor) Located in a shady corridor about a quarter mile downstream from the Transformer area on the same side of the creek. Look for the narrow slot / corridor a hundred yards or so up the hill. It seems that the Californians went home before finishing their projects, but two routes here are worthwhile. On the left wall, left to right are three unfinished projects and one completed route. Another route is on the right end of the corridor.
Magic Journey 11d/12a* The right-most bolt line.
No Self Control 11c/d** A steep line opposite Magic Journey.

INNER CIRCLE This slightly obscure rock is located south of the creek, at the edge of the meadow below the Boxtop, (see map).
Inner Circle 5.9* Climb a slab to gain a classic patina face. Four bolts plus small cams.
Friends Invited 10c* Five bolts to anchors, right of Inner Circle.

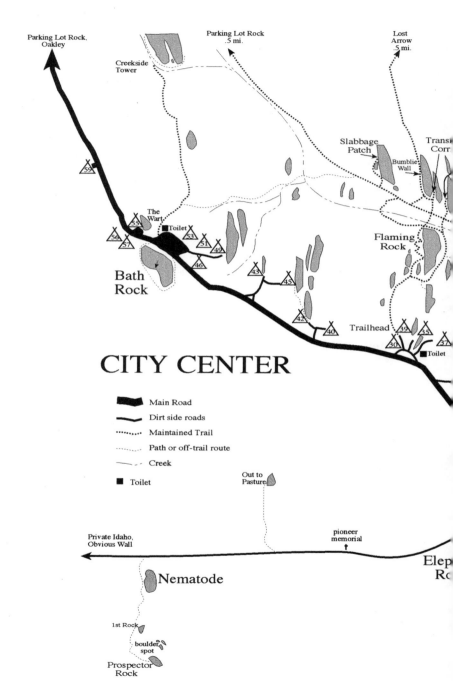

Parking Lot Rock,
Oakley

Parking Lot Rock
.5 mi.

Lost
Arrow
.5 mi.

Creekside
Tower

Slabbage
Patch

Trans
Corr

Bumblie
Wall

59

The
Wart

Toilet

Flaming
Rock

55

56

53

57

51

49

Bath
Rock

46

43

45

42

Trailhead

39

35

40

30

37

Toilet

CITY CENTER

▰▰ Main Road

━━ Dirt side roads

·········· Maintained Trail

············ Path or off-trail route

─ · ─ Creek

■ Toilet

Out to
Pasture

Private Idaho,
Obvious Wall

pioneer
memorial

Elep
Ro

Nematode

1st Rock

boulder
spot

Prospector
Rock

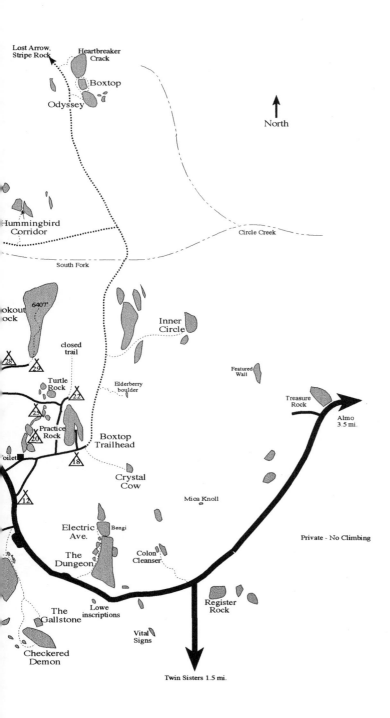

Lost Arrow,
Stripe Rock

Heartbreaker
Crack

Boxtop

Odyssey

North

Hummingbird
Corridor

Circle Creek

South Fork

6407'

ookout
ock

closed
trail

Inner
Circle

28

29

Turtle
Rock

Elderberry
boulder

Featured
Wall

Treasure
Rock

Almo
3.5 mi.

22

24

Practice
Rock

20

oilet

Boxtop
Trailhead

18

Crystal
Cow

Mica Knoll

Private - No Climbing

12

Electric
Ave.

Bengi

The
Dungeon

Colon
Cleanser

The
Gallstone

Lowe
inscriptions

Register
Rock

Checkered
Demon

Vital
Signs

Twin Sisters 1.5 mi.

BATH ROCK—ROADSIDE

Note: Most of the easier routes have little or no protection. Ratings are approximate.

A	SUNDAY MEATING 10c/d	F	STEEP START 8*
B	7	G	EASY WAY UP 4 R*
C	SOLO ROUTE 7	H	COWBOY ROUTE 4 R**
D	TYPICAL 10a	I	5 R
E	WHITE ROOF 7*	J	EASTSIDE GROOVE 6

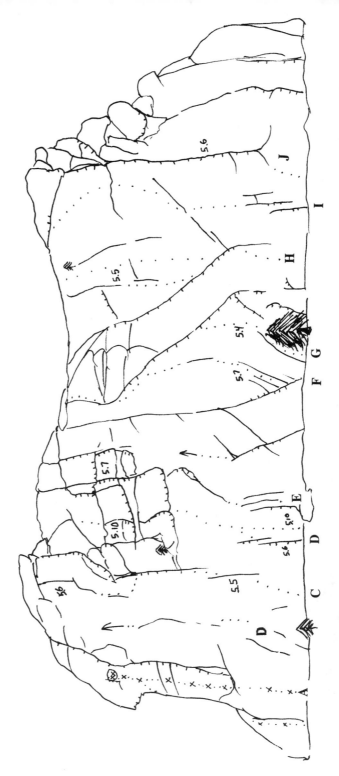

BATH ROCK—SOUTH OVERHANGS

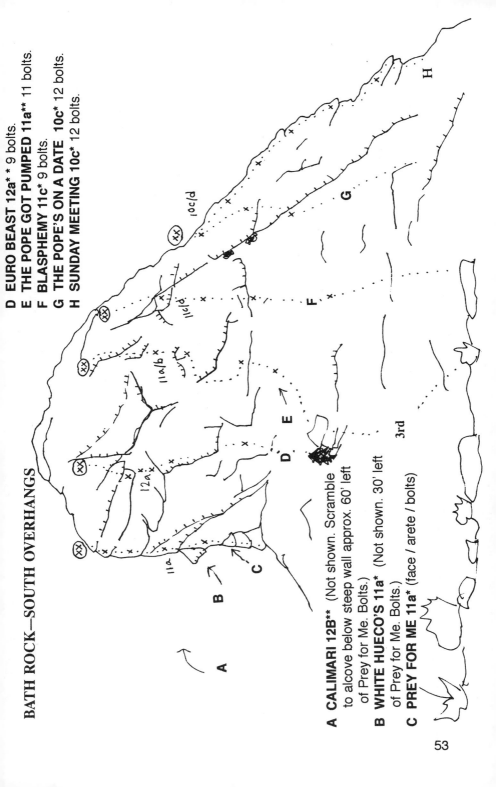

D EURO BEAST 12a* * 9 bolts.
E THE POPE GOT PUMPED 11a** 11 bolts.
F BLASPHEMY 11c* 9 bolts.
G THE POPE'S ON A DATE 10c* 12 bolts.
H SUNDAY MEETING 10c* 12 bolts.

A CALIMARI 12B** (Not shown. Scramble
to alcove below steep wall approx. 60' left
of Prey for Me. Bolts.)
B WHITE HUECO'S 11a* (Not shown. 30' left
of Prey for Me. Bolts.)
C PREY FOR ME 11a* (face / arete / bolts)

BATH ROCK - ROLLERCOASTER WALL

A BROKEN FACE 5.7R*
B PRIVATE IDAHO 5.9*
C COLLOSUS 10c**
D WILD COUNTRY 11b*
E TARANTULA 11d*
    (Runout lower section)
F LOCH NESS MONSTER 11b**
G THE WHIP 12c
    (broken hold on crux)
H DONINI'S CRACK 10c**
I COFFEE & CORNFLAKES 10a*
    (runout start)
J MAXIMUM IMPACT 11R

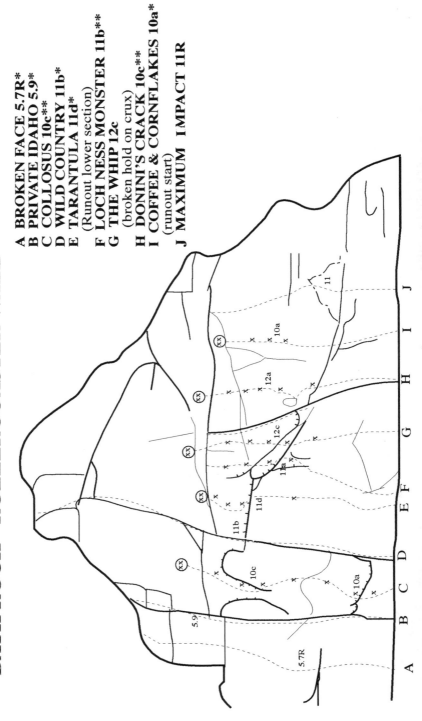

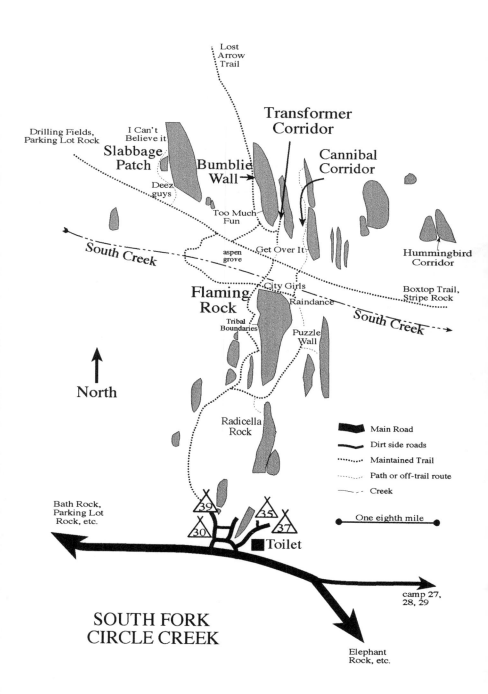

Lost Arrow Trail

Drilling Fields, Parking Lot Rock

I Can't Believe it

Transformer Corridor

Slabbage Patch

Bumblie Wall→

Cannibal Corridor

Deez guys

Too Much Fun

Get Over It

South Creek

aspen grove

Hummingbird Corridor

Boxtop Trail, Stripe Rock

City Girls

Flaming Rock

Raindance

South Creek

Tribal Boundaries

Puzzle Wall

↑ **North**

Radicella Rock

Main Road

Dirt side roads

Maintained Trail

Path or off-trail route

Creek

One eighth mile

Bath Rock, Parking Lot Rock, etc.

39
30
35
37

■ Toilet

camp 27, 28, 29

SOUTH FORK CIRCLE CREEK

Elephant Rock, etc.

FLAMING ROCK—WEST FACE

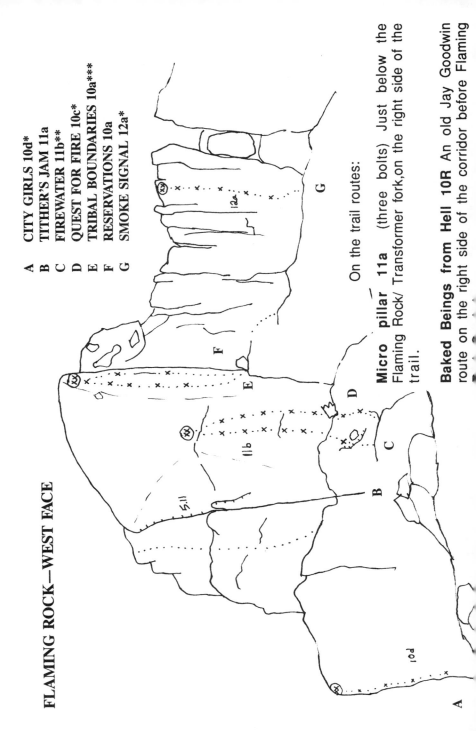

A CITY GIRLS 10d*
B TITHER'S JAM 11a
C FIREWATER 11b**
D QUEST FOR FIRE 10c*
E TRIBAL BOUNDARIES 10a***
F RESERVATIONS 10a
G SMOKE SIGNAL 12a*

On the trail routes:

Micro pillar 11a (three bolts) Just below the Flaming Rock/ Transformer fork, on the right side of the trail.

Baked Beings from Hell 10R An old Jay Goodwin route on the right side of the corridor before Flaming

FLAMING ROCK - NORTH EAST

RAINDANCE 5.7*

This climb is located approx. 100 feet left of "City Girls" on the lower (north) toe of Flaming Rock. Descend (2 ropes) the route or rap "Tribal Boundaries".

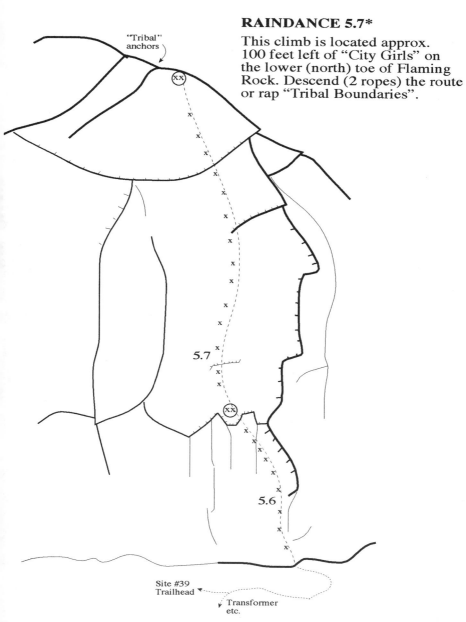

"Tribal" anchors

5.7

5.6

Site #39 Trailhead

Transformer etc.

TRANSFORMER WALL

West facing corridor north of Flaming Rock.

A **DYNAMO HUM 10c***

B **HEAT WAVE 10c****

C **VIBRATOR 10d***
(tcu's, etc.)

D **SHORT CIRCUIT 10a***

E **LIVE WIRE 10c***

F **JUST A PRETTY DAY 10a R**

CHOMPING AT THE BIT 11a**
On the wall opposite "Dynamo Hum".
Small nuts needed.

MYSTERY BOLTER 9* Slabby ridge below
"Chomping." Start in chimney.

BUMBLIE ROCK

A UNKNOWN BUMBLIE 11c*
B NEW YORK IS NOT THE CITY 10A**
C FLIGHT OF THE BUMBLIE 10a TR
D TUMBLIE TAKES A TUMBLIE 11a**

E BUMBLIE PIE 11c**
F TOO MUCH FUN 5.8***
G BUMBLIE FLAKE 5.8
H MICKI'S SIX 5.6 R*
  (look for sling anchor)
I MYSTERY BOLTER 5.9**
  (starts in Transformer Corridor)

THE SLABBAGE PATCH—WEST FACE

(Located east of Bumblie Wall)

A   HOW I spent MY SUMMER VACATION 12b*
B   THUGS IN THE GYM 13?
C   I CAN'T BELIEVE IT 10a**
D   SUCH A SLABBAGE 11b/c*
E   THE SLABBAGE PATCH 10d**
F   BEARDED SLABBAGE 10*
G   DEEZ GUYS 10a*

PRACTICE ROCK

This is the 35' west facing rock by the camping areas across from Elephant Rock. Descend off the left side.

A 5.7*
B 5.7*
C 5.7*
D FIRST LEAD 5.6**
E LITTLE PROBLEM 5.9*
F STEP LEFT 5.7*
G TOP ROPE 5.10*
H GROOVE 5.7*

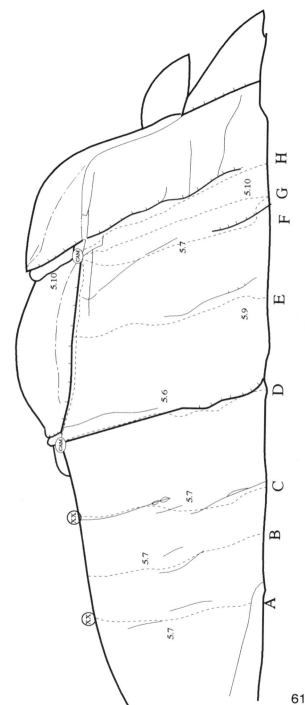

ELECTRIC AVENUE

- **A** DOGLEG 9
- **B** FRAU BLUKA 12a/b*
- **C** YOUNG FRANKENSTEIN 12a**
- **D** ELECTRIC AVENUE 11d/12a***
- **E** FIDO 11c**
- **F** SPOT 11b*
- **G** FREEWAY OF LOVE 9
- **H** SAME PLACE, DIFFERENT GIRLFRIEND 11b/c*
- **I** BENJI 12a/b**

THE DUNGEON

- **J** THE FUGITIVE (project)
- **K** LAST REQUEST 11d*
- **L** THE HERETIC 13a/b**
- **M** BALL AND CHAIN 11b**
- **N** LIFE SENTENCE 13c*
- **O** FRUIT STAND 10a

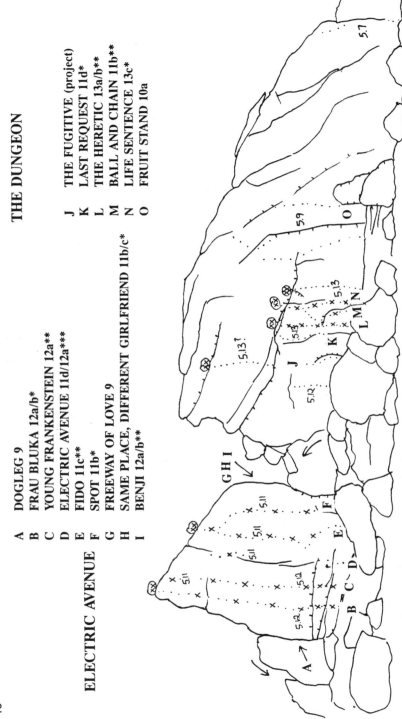

CHECKERED DEMON

Located on the W. side of the rock 200 yrds. S. of Elephant Rock.

A   RUBY AND THE DIKES 10a*
B   FACE SHOT 8 R
C   ARETE 10d
D   YONKERS 10d*
E   CHECKERED DEMON 11a**
F   SOME ASSEMBLY REQUIRED 11b**
G   TAKE A HIKE 12d**
H   GIGANTOR 13b**
I   CAPTAIN PISSGUMS 10c
J   DECLO 12 TR*
K   LUNA 12a?

ELEPHANT ROCK - NORTH SIDE

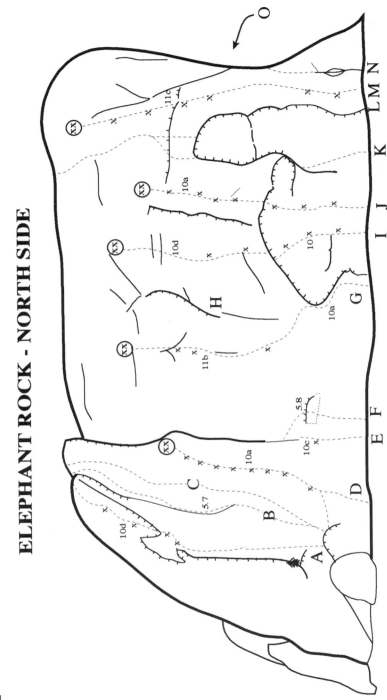

ELEPHANT ROCK - NORTH SIDE

A **POCATELLO PUNK 10D*** Solo easy rock just left of Wheat Thin to a steep bolted finish.

B **WHEAT THIN 5.7**** Climb easy rock to gain the classic thin flake that widens at the top.

C **COME ALL YE BUMBLIES 5.7** Toprope. The face just right of Wheat Thin.

D **THE PYGMIES GOT STONED 10a*** Follow bolts up the blunt arete /corner. Start with a traverse from the left, or solo directly up to the first bolt from the ground.

E **STRAWBERRY JAM 10c R** Face climb to the thin crack crux with an old bolt at your feet. Ouch.

F **STRAWBERRY SLAM 5.8 R*** Solo over the mini-roof and traverse left to finish on the Strawberry Jam crack. Scary but fairly secure.

G **BEWARE OF NESTING EGOS 11b R**** Start in the big flake or solo the direct start. Bring some small gear for this dicey classic.

H **NIGHT DEPOSIT SLOT 10a** Start in the big flake. The upper crack is seldom climbed.

I **PREPARE FOR SOARING SEAGULLS 10d*** Climb the tricky face of the big flake, then up the colorful headwall. Bring gear for the upper horizontals.

J **JUST SAY GO 10a**** Climb the bolted face to the ledge. Continue up the face past four bolts. A medium cam is helpful in the upper crack.

K **MIGHTY MUSCLE 5.9** A tricky face leads to a nasty chimney.

L **THE PEDESTAL 10c** The right side of the pedestal. Finish up the bulge and face above.

M **WERE EGOS SORE 11c*** Six bolts to chains. The crux is a mantle over the bulge.

N **THE BUMMIE 10a** Climb thru the "pod" and beyond.

O **MAURA-TORIUM 12b**** The gravely huecos on the north side. The bolts have been removed.

ELEPHANT ROCK - EAST

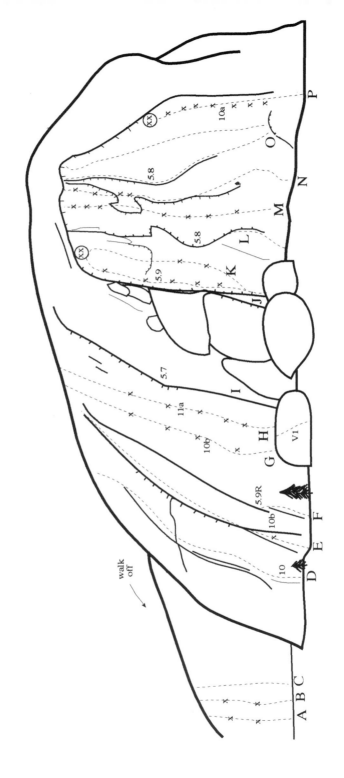

ELEPHANT ROCK - EAST

NOTE: At the time of this writing, the climbs left of "Just Say No" , including the standard walk-off descent, are private property. Most people now team up with other parties to descend the 110' rap down "Just Say No". You can also downclimb the north west side on public land, but the final 15 feet is about 5.6.

A **KISS GRANDMA 11a** A short slab with two bolts. (private property)
B **SHORT ROUTE 5.8** (private property)
C **HOT BEEF 10** Toprope.(private property)
D **WASHOUT 5.9*** A bouldery start leads to moderate climbing. (private property)
E **DISHPAN HANDS 10b** Look for the old bolt a bit off the ground. (private property)
F **WHERES THE BEEF 5.9R** Start by the juniper tree. Climb the groove to gain the major crack.
G **TRES AMIGO'S 10b*** Start on top of a boulder. A delicate slab with bolts. (private property)
H **HEIRONIMOUS BOSCH 11a*** A thinner version of Tres Amigo's. (private property)
I **COLUMBIAN CRACK 5.7***** One of the all time classsics. (private property)

J **JUST SAY NO 5.9**** One of the most popular routes at the City. Use care on the scary start.
K **SINSEMILLA 5.8R*** An old fashioned route that moves right from the start of Just Say No.
L **RYE CRISP 5.8***** The classic flake climb at the City. A bold lead for the grade.
M **PRETZEL LOGIC 10c*** A twisted bolt route just right of Rye Crisp. Bring gear for the flake.
N **POCATELLO PUNK 10d*** Solo easy rock just left of Wheat Thin to a steep, bolted finish.
O **WHEAT THIN 5.7**** Climb easy ground to gain the classic flake that widens at the top.
P **THE PYGMIES GOT STONED 10a*** The bolt line on the corner of the east and north faces.

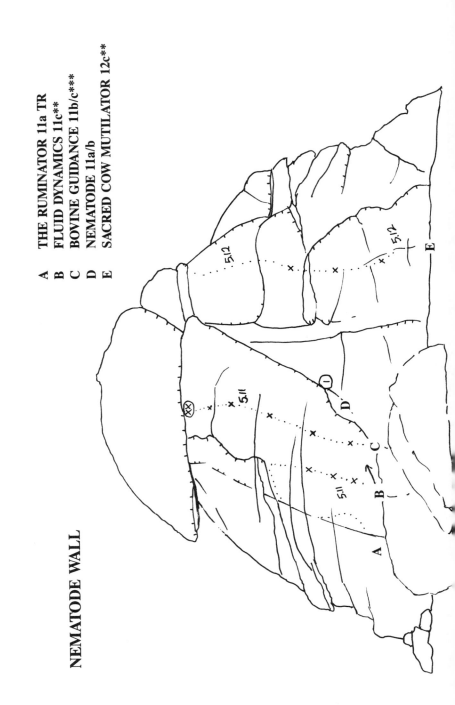

NEMATODE WALL

A THE RUMINATOR 11a TR
B FLUID DYNAMICS 11c**
C BOVINE GUIDANCE 11b/c***
D NEMATODE 11a/b
E SACRED COW MUTILATOR 12c**

OUT TO PASTURE

This small (30') rock is located
a quarter mile west of Elelpant Rock,
a hundred yds. north of the Nematode
road.

A PINSCAR 5.9
B SO MUCH FOR COOPERATION 11
C HOW NOW BROWN COW 11a*
 (long stick clip helpful)
D THIN CRACK 10d*
E BITTER ROOF 10d

CIRCLE CREEK VALLEY

The Circle Creek Valley is by far the largest area described in this book, and includes the lowland meadows around **The Dolphin**, **The Boxtop**, and **The Lost Arrow**, as well as the developing crags around the **North Fork of Circle Creek**. Until recently, the only access was a substantial walk from the Flaming Rock trailhead or the trail from Practice Rock. With the addition of the Circle Creek overlook road (see map) , crags like **Building Blocks**, **Stripe Rock**, **The Great Wall**, etc. are now a much closer walk.

Another new access, the North Fork trail starts at the Upper Breadloaves, climbs to the head of the Circle Creek Valley, then drops past many undeveloped rocks on it's way to connect with the Stripe Rock trail. Though closed to bikes, this is a beautiful hike or run and promises to open up many hidden crags. Unfortunately, the City's premiere sport crag, the Dolphin, is still very much on private land, with little hope of future access. Check out the following routes not shown in topo's.

TOMMY KNOCKER / LADY JANE These two short, bolted routes are on a rock just left of the new Bumblie - Lost Arrow trail. (see map on page 76) The left route, **Lady Jane**, is about **5.7** and the right **Tommy Knocker** is about **10a**.

JODEEN BOULDER This is the big boulder that sits by the Lost Arrow's northwest side.
Forcash and Riches 11a* Four bolts on a nice short face.

BUSH PIG On the right side of the trail between the Lost Arrow and The Building Blocks, this small rock is on private land.
Grey Son 10a* A bouldery move, traverse left and up. Bolts.
Bush Pig 11d** On the northeast side. Four bolts.

WHINING ROCK This slightly obscured rock has a very nice north-west face. Just west of Stripe Rock, the rock is set back from the trail, behind another rock formation. There is potential for more routes here.
Cruel and Unusual Whining 11b** Seven bolts on the steep, patina face.

ORANGE WALL Set back in the hobbit lands east of the Lost Arrow, look for the arch feature with orange lichen.
Filer's Crack 5.9* This is the clean four inch crack on the orange east face.
Arch 5.10? Has anyone done this?

SLASH ROCK Just north and a little west of Stripe rock, this rock has a diagonally grooved east side with several moderate possibilities, but only one recorded route.
Do-Do Drive 5.9+ (1980 rating) A diagonal flake on the right side of the rock, with a hard start.

BUCKETLAND A group of rocks on the north side of the road across from Building Blocks. Approach from the new overlook road.
Bucket Land 10a* On the west side. A steep start, a low angle bit, finishing steep to an anchor.
Jug City 5.9* Right of Bucketland.
Pine-Tina 10a* To the right of the other routes. Use Bucketland anchors for descent.

GEOWATT - See map for location. Find two routes on the west side of a boxtop type rock, north of the overlook road.
Left Geowatt 10a* Four bolts to anchors.
Right Geowatt 10c to 11d*, depending on start. Four bolts to anchors.

GREY WALL This big west face is set back to the east, above the The North Fork Trail. A possible site of multi- pitch routes, this wall is within a federally designated "Research Natural Area", where cattle are allowed but people are not. Hmmm.

BEEF JELLO CRAG A trail to this outback area has been flagged, cutting right (north) of the new loop trail, about a quarter mile up from Stripe Rock. Probably about a 30 minute walk up from Stripe Rock.
Beef Jello 10d** Perhaps one of the best crack climbs at the City. Bring cams to 3.5".
The Mould 13 Project? Left of Beef Jello.

FIESTA SPIRE A small tower with some nice crack routes, located at about 7,000' in the top of the creek drainage, just east of the trail. Approach via the North Fork Trail from the Upper Breadloaves.
Piñata 10a* Skirt the left side of the north face.
Dancin' on Diamonds 10a* Crack.
Fiesta 10b** Crack.
Tickled Pink 5.9+R Wander carefully up the west face.

CRESCENT CRAG An out-of-the-way adventure destination. See Circle Creek map. Best approached as for Fiesta Spire.
Crescent Crack 10a* A prominent crack on the west side with rap anchor.
Toprope 10* To the right of Crescent Crack.
Red Dihedral 12a* TR Down and right of Crescent Crack.

JIM'S JEWEL This rock is rumored to be "directly east of Banana Buttress".
Jim's Jewel 5.7* A 120' obvious crack on the west face.
Diamond Grinder 5.9* The off-width crack right of Jim's Jewel.

PRECAMBRIAN ZONE
Roadmap Wall, Granite Mountain and Stienfell's Dome are part of the ridge that forms the northeast side of the Circle Creek drainage. This ridge is of Pre-Cambrian origin, and has been dated as some of the oldest exposed rocks on earth, at around 2.5 billion years old. Climbing on this rock is different than most of the City, with fewer protection cracks, no faces of brown patina, and a much coarser rock with large crystals. The recently built overlook road accesses this huge area of relatively unexplored climbing potential.

ROADMAP WALL The big west face with criss-crossed white dikes, about a quarter mile west of Stienfell's Dome. The only route is a scary looking Greg Lowe route from the early 1970's.

Roadmap West Face 5.10? A prominent flake system in the center of the face. Start at a small roof.

THE APRON While driving from the main Almo road to the Circle Creek Overlook, look to the right to spot this wild overhang on the west side of a rock.

Darius, Tedd and Tony's Route 12d? (open project)

LITTLE THUMB In the Pre-Cambrian zone east of Stienfell's Dome, this rock can be approached from the circle creek overlook parking area. Contour right below the rocks then up a minor drainage. Little
Thumb is on the left.

North Side 10a*
Whorl 11c top-rope
Thumbs Up 5.9 A-2
Unnamed 10d
The Facet 11a* A small rock uphill and right from Little Thumb has a single four bolt route to anchors.

MURO ROJO This crag can be seen in the saddle on top of the precambrian ridge, east of Steinfell's and Little Thumb. Approach from the "snakepit" parking lot (an old gravel pit), a couple hundred yards east of the overlook / Almo road junction. Follow the flagged trail, then go left on the old road to a drainage which leads up to the saddle.

Feisty 11c* Four bolts to anchors on the left side of the wall.
Red Hook 11c* One bolt and gear crack.
Ready or Not 10b* A crack line right of Red Hook.
Brad's 5.8 Further right.

THE BLADE A prominent facet of steep rock on the hillside above the Almo road. Two aid routes tackle the main wall. To the right is a lonely free route.

Once Bitten 5.10a The big crack right of **Twice Shy 5.10 C2** and **The Blade 5.9 A2.**

ROCK ONE The first crag of interest as you drive up the road from Almo. This is the diamond-shaped feature east of The Blade. This looks promising from the road, but is not very climber friendly.

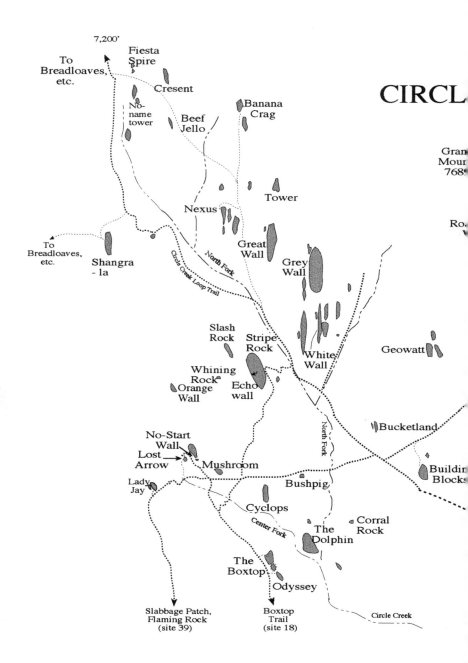

7,200'

To Breadloaves, etc.

Fiesta Spire

Cresent

No-name tower

Beef Jello

Banana Crag

CIRCL

Gran Moun 768

Ro

Tower

Nexus

To Breadloaves, etc.

Shangra - la

Circle Creek Loop Trail

North Fork

Great Wall

Grey Wall

Slash Rock

Stripe Rock

Whining Rock

Orange Wall

Echo wall

White Wall

Geowatt

Bucketland

North Fork

No-Start Wall

Lost Arrow

Mushroom

Lady Jay

Bushpig

Building Blocks

Cyclops

Center Fork

The Dolphin

Corral Rock

The Boxtop

Odyssey

Slabbage Patch, Flaming Rock (site 39)

Boxtop Trail (site 18)

Circle Creek

CREEK BASIN

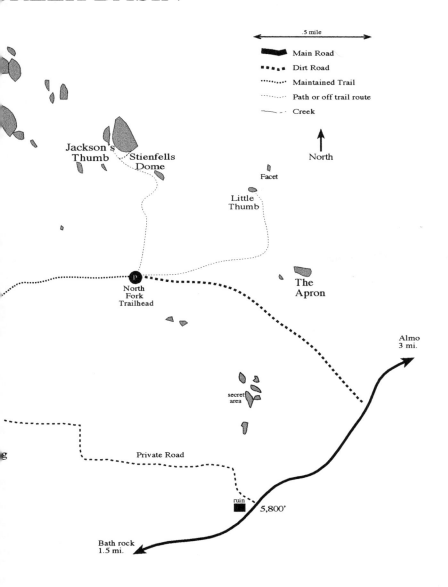

.5 mile

Main Road
Dirt Road
Maintained Trail
Path or off trail route
Creek

North

Jackson's
Thumb   Stienfells
            Dome

Facet

Little
Thumb

North
Fork
Trailhead

The
Apron

Almo
3 mi.

Private Road

secret
area

ruin   5,800'

Bath rock
1.5 mi.

ODYSSEY

A   WHY BE NORMAL 11b
B   ODYSSEY 12a**
C   PIGEON CRACK 11d
D   DRIVING AT NIGHT 9**
E   HALF MOON 10d
F   HANG TEN 10a*
G   JUST ANOTHER MORMON ON DRUGS 10
H   THIS IS NOT MY BEAUTIFUL WIFE 11a
I   OUCH 11a

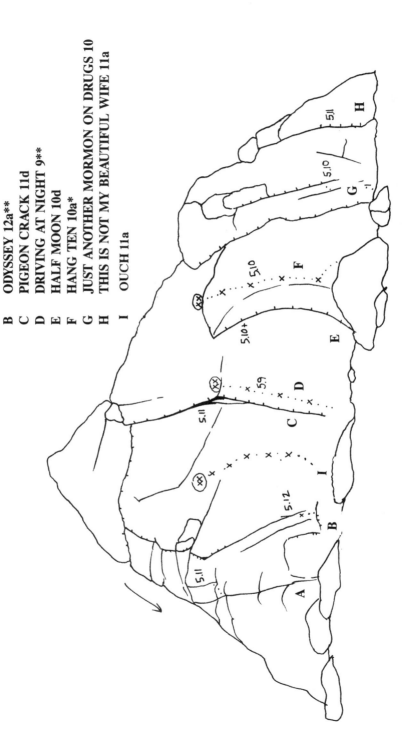

THE BOXTOP–EAST

Descent: Rap off
summit block
then scramble
down chim. on
e. side.

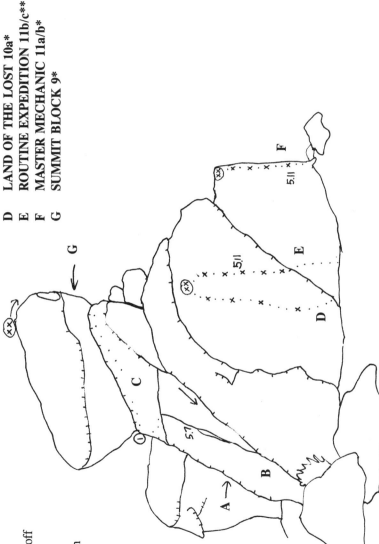

A **CORRIDOR CRACK 8***
  (start in chimney)
B **BOXTOP TRAVERSE 9***
C **CRACK–FACE 7**
D **LAND OF THE LOST 10a***
E **ROUTINE EXPEDITION 11b/c****
F **MASTER MECHANIC 11a/b***
G **SUMMIT BLOCK 9***

HEARTBREAKER

Northwest Face
This rock is located just east of the Lost Arrow trail, about 1/8 mile north of the Boxtop.

A **HEARTBREAKER 10c***** Classic hand crack.
B **JAY'S PROJECT 12?**
C **SURFING THE ORGASMIC WAVE 11b****
Bring small nuts, etc.
D **OPEN Y-D 5.7***

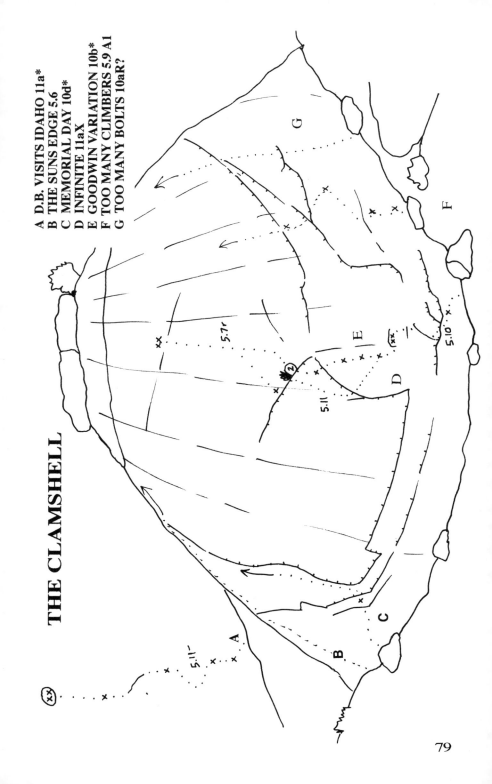

THE CLAMSHELL

A D.B. VISITS IDAHO 11a*
B THE SUNS EDGE 5.6
C MEMORIAL DAY 10d*
D INFINITE 11aX
E GOODWIN VARIATION 10b*
F TOO MANY CLIMBERS 5.9 A1
G TOO MANY BOLTS 10aR?

THE LOST ARROW

Two ropes required for rap.

A DYING FOR EXPOSURE 5.8x
B THE CLASSIC ROUTE 5.7***
   (Requires gear anchor.)
C THE ROPE THIEF 11R
D ISCHEMIC PAIN 12a**
E FISTS OF FURY 11

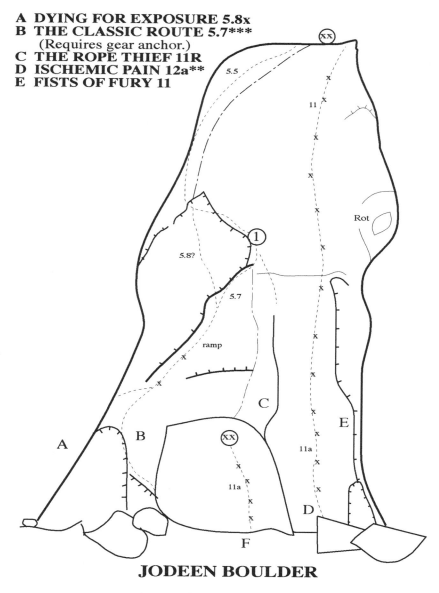

JODEEN BOULDER

F FORCASH AND RICHES 11a*

NO START WALL

A SQUEEZEBOX 10d offwidth
B BOSS HOG 12b
C VERTICAL TURTLE 9r* A classic.
D SIZZLER 12a* direct start to Big Pig
E BIG PIG 10d** A long traversing pitch
    on big holds.
F BABE C-2 (aid) 5.11?
G POWER PIG 12a** Short but fun.
H SOUTH RIB 5.9* bolts & gear.

Note: Stick clip required on Boss Hog,
Sizzler and Big Pig.

MUSHROOM ROCK

A NORTH SLAB LEFT 5.7*
B NORTH SLAB RIGHT 5.9*
C SEA BISCUIT 12C**
D MARGIN WALKER 11C*

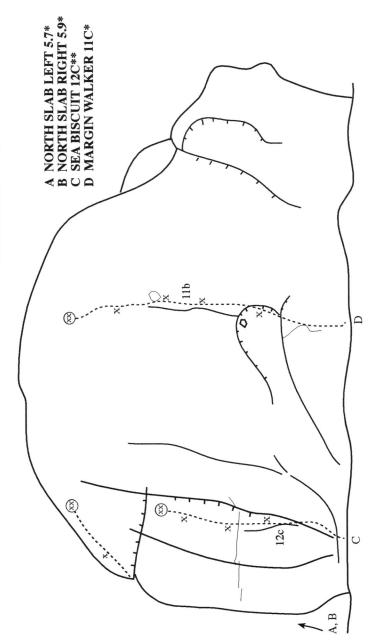

CYCLOPS - A.K.A. MEADOW MUFFIN

There are many options for moderate, poorly protected, mossy routes on this rock.

A TOO COOL FOR THE COBBLER 11b*
B UNDER TOUCAN'S NOSE 11a*
C MAVIS 5.5 *
D CYCLOPS SCRAMBLE *

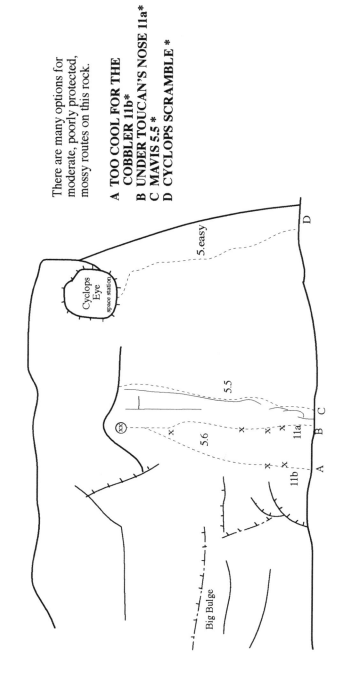

BUILDING BLOCKS

Some of the City's best !

A ZIP DRIVE 11a* Short & cranky.

B RASTUS 11c Dicey mixed gear & bolts.

C TECHNOWEENIE 11a/b** Very fun.
Protect the diagonal crack w/ medium pro, then bolts.

D TECHNOCOLOR 12b** A '87 Yaniro testpiece that
follows the clean arete.

E TECHNICON 11d** Follow TCU crack
to thin traverse / arete. Super route.

F SCRAPS 11a* 1st route right of arete. Bolts & gear.

G DROPZONE 10d Thin, early 80's gear route.

H LEGO 5.9/10a** Start on boulder. A bolt journey
on big plates.

I VICEGRIPS 11? A late 60's Greg Lowe route.

J STEREOTYPIC BEHAVIOR 10d Natural pro on
steep plates.

K ACID RAIN 10a* Climb 20' to first bolt.

EAST SIDE - left to right (not shown)

L THE MECHANIC 11d* Climb the brown fin, past
sparse bolts.

M RAINGUTTER 11? An old Lowe route.

N THE MILKMAN 11g Impossible looking slab
with big ring bolts. Yaniro.

O PEAPOD 11? Another old Lowe route.

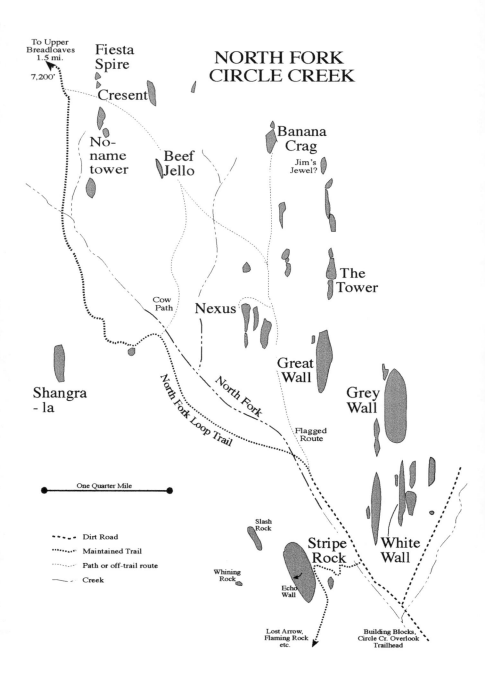

NORTH FORK
CIRCLE CREEK

To Upper
Breadloaves
1.5 mi.

7,200'

Fiesta
Spire

Cresent

No-
name
tower

Beef
Jello

Banana
Crag

Jim's
Jewel?

The
Tower

Cow
Path

Nexus

Great
Wall

Grey
Wall

Shangra
- la

North Fork

North Fork Loop Trail

Flagged
Route

One Quarter Mile

Slash
Rock

Stripe
Rock

White
Wall

Whining
Rock

Echo
Wall

- - - - Dirt Road

.... Maintained Trail

.... Path or off-trail route

— Creek

Lost Arrow,
Flaming Rock
etc.

Building Blocks,
Circle Cr. Overlook
Trailhead

86

STRIPE ROCK - WEST
ECHO WALL

A BOUNCE 10c*
B SONIC BOOM 10b
(some gear required)
C SHOCK WAVES 10d*

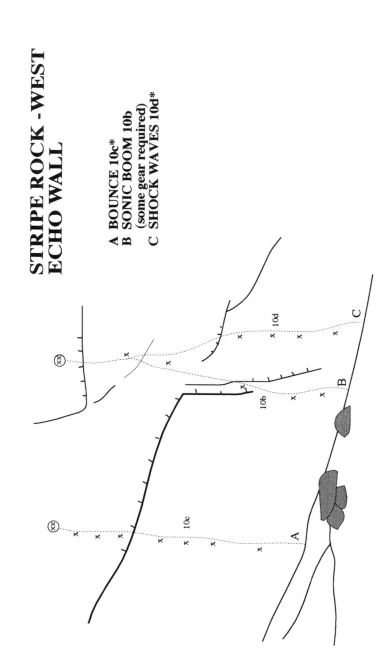

STRIPE ROCK

Approach: The easiest route is a flat one mile walk from the Circle Creek Overlook trailhead.

Descent: From the top of Cruel Shoes, walk left toward the top of the white aplite dike, then west down a ramp to find a two rope rappell down the west side.

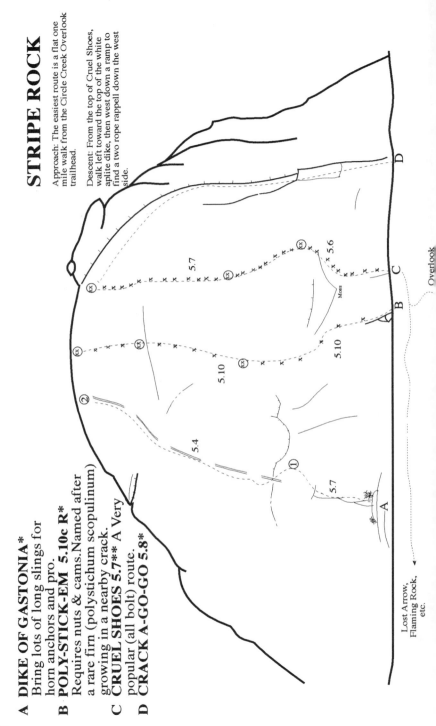

5.7

5.6

Moss

5.10

5.10

5.4

5.7

Overlook

Lost Arrow,
Flaming Rock,
etc.

A **DIKE OF GASTONIA***
   Bring lots of long slings for
   horn anchors and pro.

B **POLY-STICK-EM 5.10c R***
   Requires nuts & cams.Named after
   a rare firn (polystichum scopulinum)
   growing in a nearby crack.

C **CRUEL SHOES 5.7*** A Very
   popular (all bolt) route.

D **CRACK A-GO-GO 5.8***

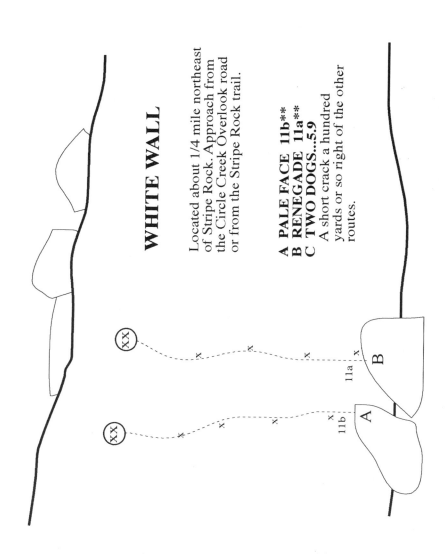

WHITE WALL

Located about 1/4 mile northeast of Stripe Rock. Approach from the Circle Creek Overlook road or from the Stripe Rock trail.

A PALE FACE 11b**
B RENEGADE 11a**
C TWO DOGS...5.9
A short crack a hundred yards or so right of the other routes.

THE GREAT WALL
west face

2 pitch trad routes.

A YEEHAW 5.9+ R*
B YAHOO 5.9*
C MODELO 5.8*

Anchor locations approximate.

THE NEXUS
northwest face

A SKIP IT 10b
B VORTEX 5.9*
C CLIP IT 11D**
D ANOTHER BUCKET SLAVE 12b***
E GET SCRAPPY 10c

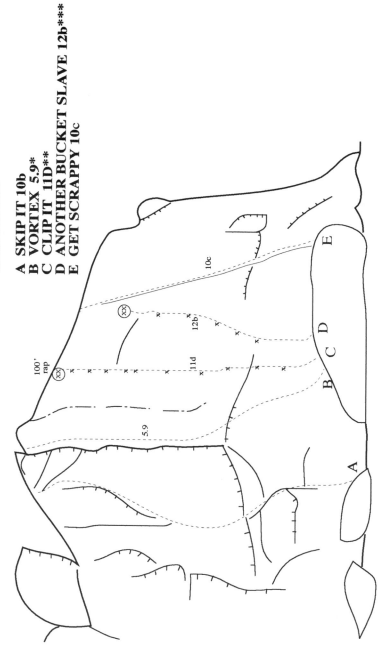

BANANA BUTTRESS

east face

A BANANA PEEL 5.9** bolts.
B BANANA BELLY 5.9**
 bolts and gear.
C BANANA BELT 5.9 crack
D BANANA SPLIT 10d*
 bolts and gear.

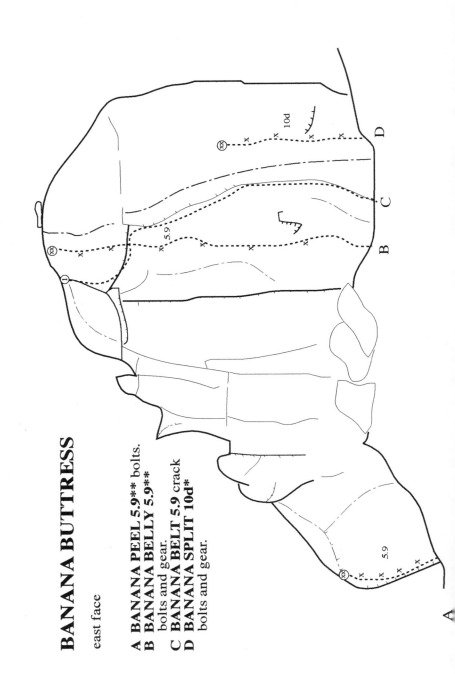

STEINFELLS DOME

JACKSON'S THUMB

A THEATER OF SHADOWS 5.7** (fully bolted)
B WEST FACE 5.9/ 5.10R (several routes)
C ORANGE CRACK 5.10d
D SOUTH BUTTRESS 5.8

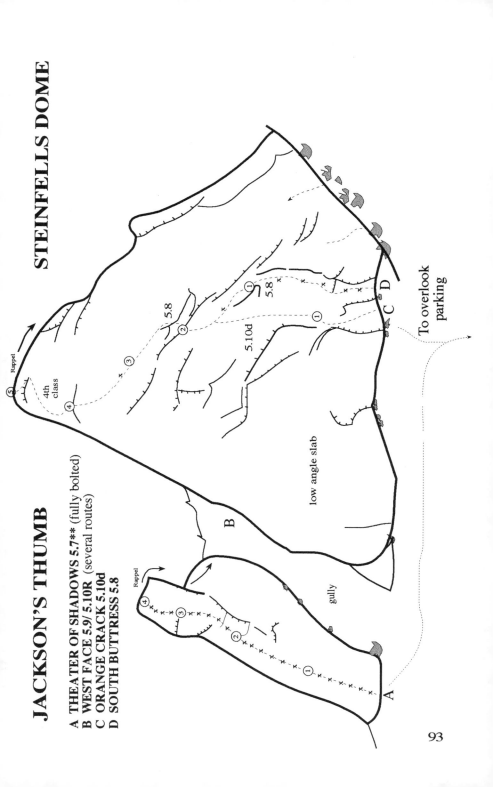

To overlook
parking

93

TWIN SISTERS

Separated from the main City of Rocks by about two miles of dirt road, the Twin Sisters are the largest rock formations at the City, with the exception of Stienfell's Dome. Running roughly in a north - south direction, the Sisters are the high point of a ridge that has dozens of impressive rocks and over a hundred established climbs. Several routes on the North Sister are among the City's best, offering three pitch routes on excellent rock. Unfortunately, the National Park Service has chosen to close climbing on the Twin Sisters themselves due to perceived climber "impairment" of what they call the "Historic View Shed". I have included climbs in this area because the chances of re-opening the closed areas are promising.

The other problem here is that much of the rest of the climbing is privately owned. Unlike the owners of the Dolphin, etc, the Sisters' landowner has long been tolerant of climbers who don't scare his cattle or leave gates open. He owns a new cabin on the east side of the ridge, and visiting climbers have received permission to climb.

Despite problems, it's still worthwhile to climb in the Sisters area, as open classics like **BLM Corridor**, **Bulldog Wall, White Lightning** and **Yellow Wall** are a lot of fun. Access to climbs on the west side of the Sisters, **Skinner's Roof**, **Weather Wall, Yellow Wall** and **Secret Toms** is made via the private ranch road that leaves the main road a hundred yards south of the picnic area. The landowner seems fine with slow-speed driving out this road as long as gates are left closed.

SECRET TOM'S Drive or walk out the west side road past the water trough, turning right at a fork. Park close to a formation with a prominent right arête. This is **End of the Affair 12c/d**.** Continue up the hill to Secret Tom's formation with a big left facing dihedral.
West with the Night 11c** On the left end, just around the corner from the main face. Nice rock.
Crisco 11b/c Obvious crack with bolts starting 30' off the ground.
Calling All Bumblies 12b* Climb the wild dihedral.
Sanguine Slug 11a Chossy rock with bolts right of "Calling All Bumblies". No hangers?
Payson 11d* The arching half-moon crack. Bolts and natural pro.
The Secretion 10b A crack climb right of Payson.

MISSISSIPPI FREDS Fred was a homeless fellow living on the streets of Ketchum, Idaho in the early 80s. He carried his gear in a red bandanna on the end of a stick. The climb is a wide 5.9 crack line on a rock a bit west of Yellow Wall.

NEEDLE ROCK Can be seen from the main road on the east side of the Sisters ridge. Just left is Northwall. Rumor has it that the needle is about to topple so stay away!

BFD ROCK The first rock south of the picnic area with the steep west face above an outhouse. The east side is directly above the road.
The Smell 12c** The bolted face above the outhouse. This route is said to be stiff for the grade.
Killing Time 5.8 Top-rope? On the East side, above the road. Left of the central crack, start on a boulder and climb past a small roof.
Central Crack 5.7 Kind of a thrash.
Mr. Magoo 5.9 Top-rope? Right of the central crack, up a face past two roofs.

THE FLINTSTONE Three hard routes on really good rock are located on a steep wave up around the corner (to the right) and up from Picnic Dome.
Betty 12c/d** The right hand route. Bolts and gear.
Bam-Bam 12b/c*** Center route. Burly.
Rubble Without a Cause 11c On the right side.

THE INDIAN CHIEF This is the rock on the east side of the road, across from BFD Rock. There are lots of options for easy to moderate (5.6 -5.9) climbs on the east side.

Close to the Edge 12c* On an outcrop east of the picnic area, look for bolts on an arete with quartz rock at the start.

AMERICAN EAGLE The distinctive rock just east of the road, north of the Indian Chief. **Scott Fry's Project**. Check out these whisker-thin cracks on the left end of west side.

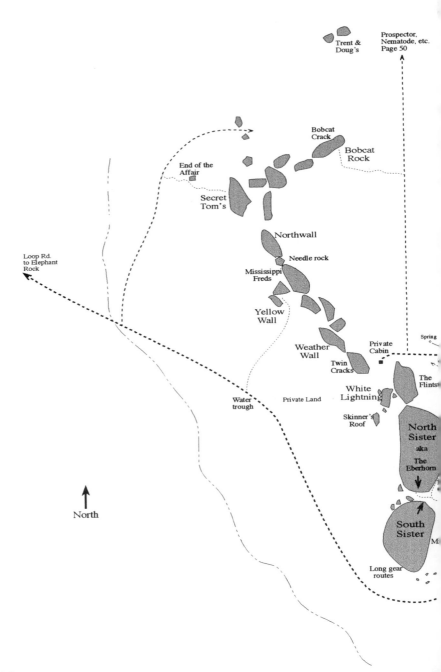

Trent &
Doug's

Prospector,
Nematode, etc.
Page 50

Bobcat
Crack

Bobcat
Rock

End of the
Affair

Secret
Tom's

Northwall

Needle rock

Mississippi
Freds

Loop Rd.
to Elephant
Rock

Yellow
Wall

Weather
Wall

Private
Cabin

Spring

Twin
Cracks

The
Flints

White
Lightning

Skinner's
Roof

North
Sister

aka

The
Eberhorn

Water
trough

Private Land

North

South
Sister

M

Long gear
routes

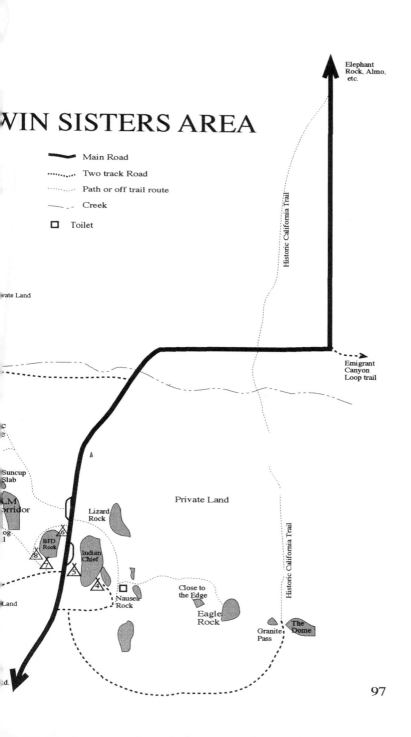

WIN SISTERS AREA

— Main Road

.... Two track Road

.... Path or off trail route

— . — Creek

☐ Toilet

Elephant Rock, Almo, etc.

Historic California Trail

Emigrant Canyon Loop trail

vate Land

Private Land

Suncup Slab

M orridor

og.

Lizard Rock

BFD Rock

Indian Chief

Nausea Rock

Close to the Edge

Eagle Rock

Granite Pass

The Dome

Historic California Trail

Land

d.

97

THE EBERHORN—HIGHER TWIN SISTER

CLOSED

A STATIC CLING 11c**
B AID CORNER 12?
C 11/12?
D FLAKE ROUTE 11
E BALCONY ROUTE 10b**
F N.E. SHOULDER 7

Descent: Rap Static cling, NE shoulder
or S. face.

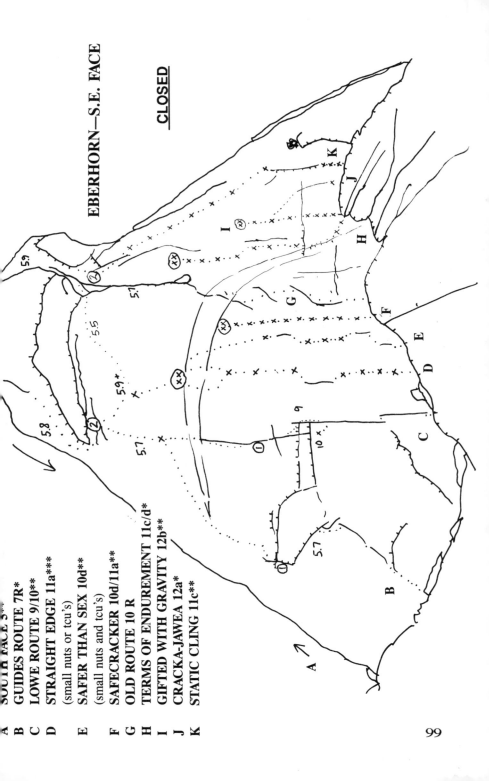

EBERHORN—S.E. FACE

CLOSED

A   SOUTH FACE 5***
B   GUIDES ROUTE 7R*
C   LOWE ROUTE 9/10**
D   STRAIGHT EDGE 11a***
    (small nuts or tcu's)
E   SAFER THAN SEX 10d**
    (small nuts and tcu's)
F   SAFECRACKER 10d/11a**
G   OLD ROUTE 10 R
H   TERMS OF ENDUREMENT 11c/d*
I   GIFTED WITH GRAVITY 12b**
J   CRACKA-JAWEA 12a*
K   STATIC CLING 11c**

99

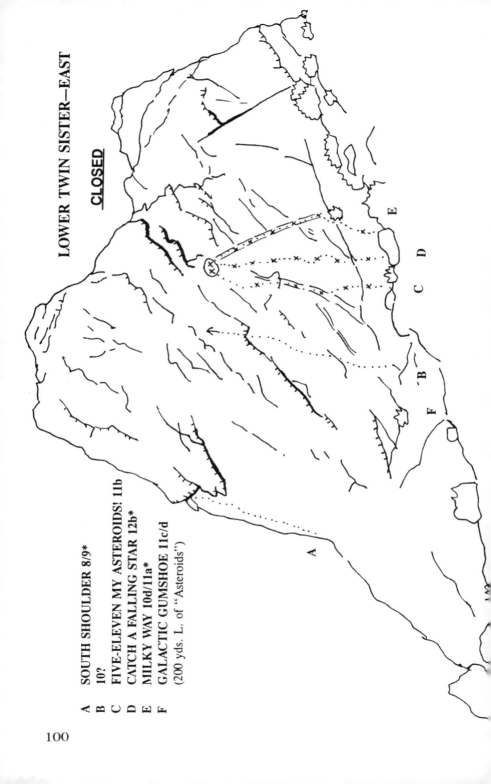

LOWER TWIN SISTER—EAST

CLOSED

A   SOUTH SHOULDER 8/9*
B   10?
C   FIVE-ELEVEN MY ASTEROIDS! 11b
D   CATCH A FALLING STAR 12b*
E   MILKY WAY 10d/11a*
F   GALACTIC GUMSHOE 11c/d
    (200 yds. L. of "Asteroids")

Descent: Rap and downclimb
Northeast end.

A NEW ROUTE 11?
B TENNY'S ROUTE 9 R
C OLD WEST FACE 9 R*
D SOUTH SHOULDER 8/9

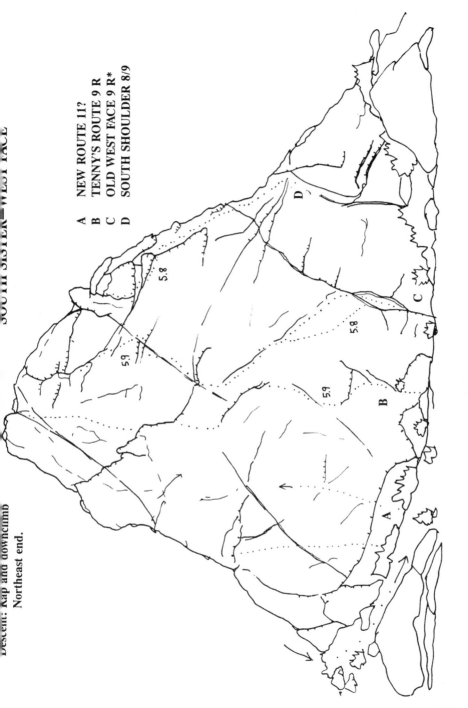

BLM ROCK—WEST CORRIDOR

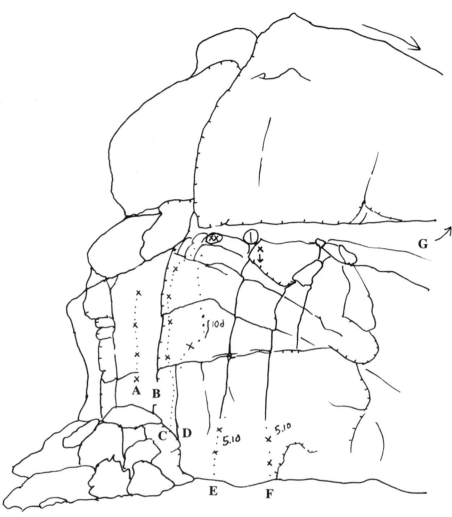

A   **BOGGS-COSTELLO MEMORIAL 11b***
B   **CRACK 9**
C   **WHERE RANGERS RETIRE 10c****
D   **DO RANGERS DREAM OF ELECTRIC SHEEP?**
      10d**
E   **THE RANGER'S A PSYCHO 10b/c****
F   **GOOD ENOUGH FOR GOVERNMENT WORK**
      10c**
G   **DON'T BE A GUBERIF 10**
      (roof crack)

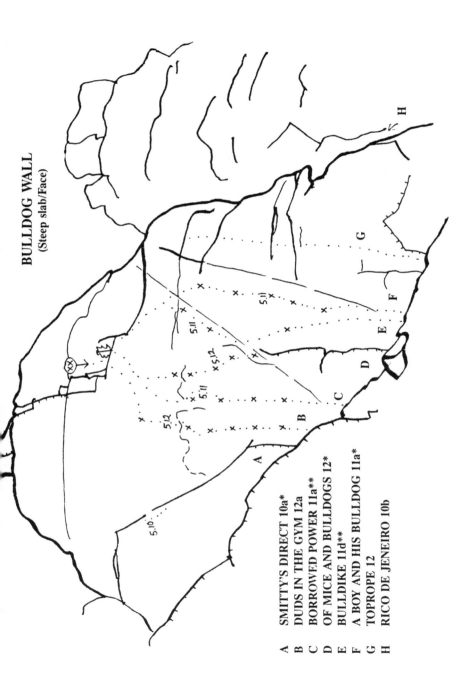

BULLDOG WALL
(Steep slab/Face)

A   SMITTY'S DIRECT 10a*
B   DUDS IN THE GYM 12a
C   BORROWED POWER 11a**
D   OF MICE AND BULLDOGS 12*
E   BULLDIKE 11d**
F   A BOY AND HIS BULLDOG 11a*
G   TOPROPE 12
H   RICO DE JENEIRO 10b

103

SUNCUP SLAB

(OUTHOUSE SLAB)

A SHIT IN THE WOODS 5.8R
B PUCKER FACTOR 10dx
C EASY MOVEMENTS 5.5*
D SUNCUP SLAB 5.8*
  (direct – 5.9R)
E SLAB CLIMBING 102 5.7R
F SUNCUP CRACK 5.4

BLM CORRIDOR

PICNIC DOME

THE FLINTSTONE

BETTY 12c/d**
BAM-BAM 12b/c***
RUBBLE WITHOUT A CAUSE 11a

A   CRACK/FACE 10a
B   BRIGHTON BEACH 10a
C   HOLIDAYS IN THE SUN 10b*

NAUSEA WALL

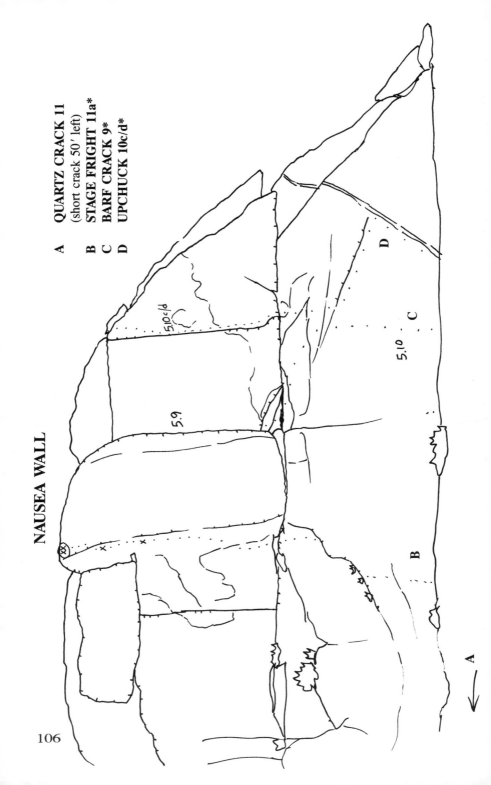

A **QUARTZ CRACK 11**
   (short crack 50′ left)
B **STAGE FRIGHT 11a***
C **BARF CRACK 9***
D **UPCHUCK 10c/d***

5.9

5.10c/d

5.10

106

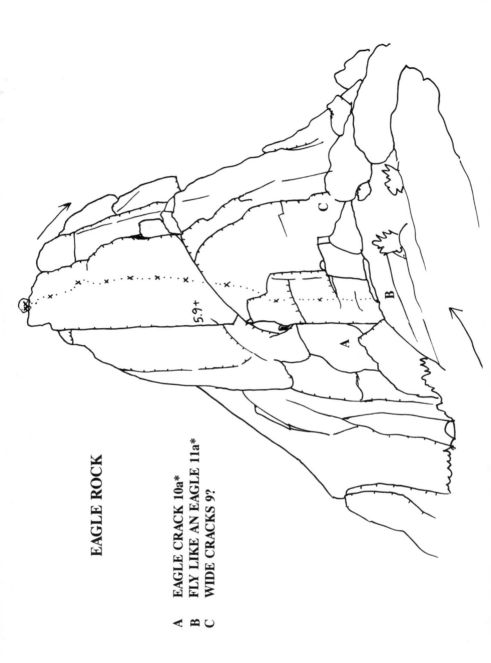

EAGLE ROCK

A EAGLE CRACK 10a*
B FLY LIKE AN EAGLE 11a*
C WIDE CRACKS 9?

WEATHER WALL

A   **SQUALL LINE 10b** (arete l. of chimney)
B   **OH HAIL! 11a** (face r. of chimney)
C   **FORCASTINATION 11a** (face and leaning dihedral)
D   **FIRE AND GRIMSTONE 11c**
E   **THUNDER RIDGE 10a**
F   **STORM FRONT 11b**** (mixed bolts and crack pro, center of prow)
G   **HIGH PRESSURE SYSTEM 10a**** (r. side of prow)
H   **TWIN CRACKS 9** (two pitches) (obvious cracks on formation S.W. of Weather Wall)

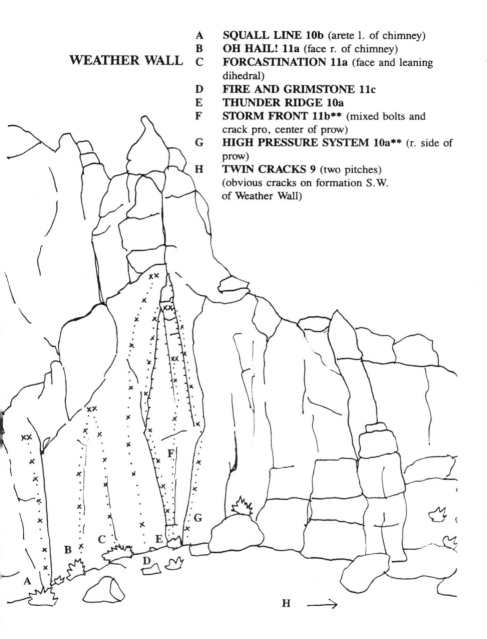

These routes can be found on the north
facing outcrops just N. of the Sisters.

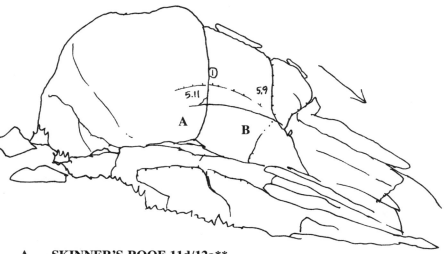

A   **SKINNER'S ROOF 11d/12a****
B   **MARGARINE FINGERS 9**
C   **WHITE LIGHTNING 10b****
        LITTLE YELLOW MAN 11c*

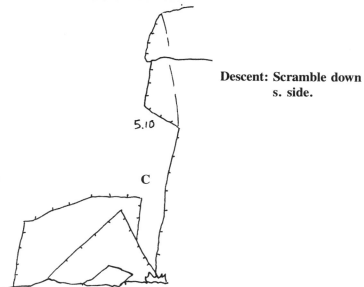

**Descent: Scramble down
s. side.**

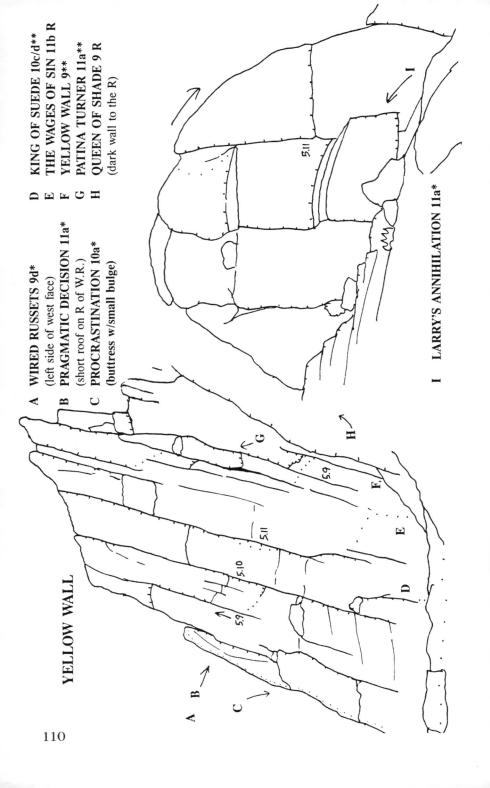

YELLOW WALL

A WIRED RUSSETS 9d*
(left side of west face)
B PRAGMATIC DECISION 11a*
(short roof on R of W.R.)
C PROCRASTINATION 10a*
(buttress w/small bulge)

D KING OF SUEDE 10c/d**
E THE WAGES OF SIN 11b R
F YELLOW WALL 9**
G PATINA TURNER 11a**
H QUEEN OF SHADE 9 R
(dark wall to the R)

I LARRY'S ANNIHILATION 11a*

5.11
5.10
5.9
5.9

NORTHWALL

A **ROTTEN OFFWIDTH 10**
B **DARKEST IDAHO 9**
C **JAWS 9**
D **TOPROPE 8/9**
E **10?**

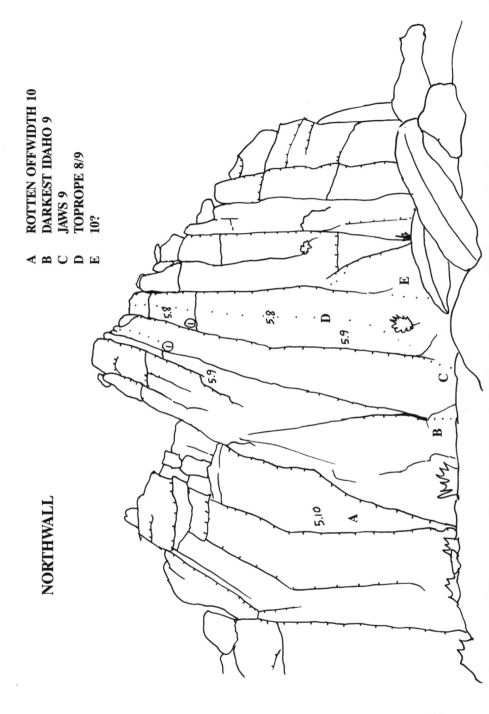

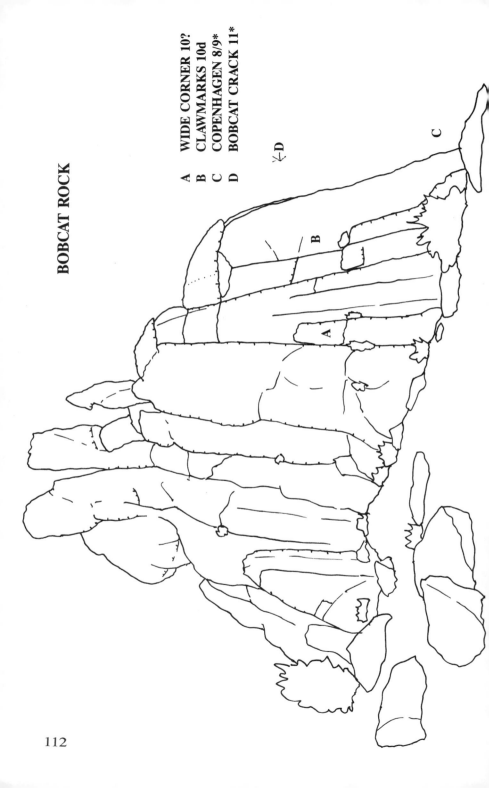

BOBCAT ROCK

A WIDE CORNER 10?
B CLAWMARKS 10d
C COPENHAGEN 8/9*
D BOBCAT CRACK 11*

SECRET TOM'S

A **WEST WITH THE NIGHT 11c****
B **CRISCO 11c** Bolts and gear
C **CALLING ALL BUMBLIES 12c***
D **SANGUINE SLUG** 11a no hangers?
E **PAYSON 11d***

F **END OF THE AFFAIR 12c/d****
   Located on smaller formation between
   Secret Tom's and the road.

Approach: continue on the road
past the Yellow Wall area, staying
right at a fork. Park when the crag
comes into view on the ridge to the
right (east).

CAMPING

There are currently seventy-eight designated campsites in the City of Rocks National Reserve. Each site costs $7.00 per night and allows a maximum of two vehicles and up to eight people. Extra vehicles are charged $5.00 per night.

Eight sites are closed for various reasons, and twenty-two are designated "walk in" sites. That leaves only forty-eight sites for "car camping", with twenty-four of those earmarked as RV suitable sites. In most cases, the walk in sites are still quite close to parking, and it is o.k. to sleep in your vehicle.

The big change has been the introduction of a reservation system where one can call in and reserve a site up to two days in advance. The park officials leave only 25% of the sites open for non-reserved campers, so it's advisable to make that call and pay the $6.00 reservation fee, especially on weekends.

If you arrive without a reserved site, you will first need to locate an open site, then pick up a pay envelope at Bath Rock, then return to place the stub on the campsite marker.

Group sites are available, but for my money it seems better to book adjacent sites (that allow eight people per site). That's a choice between $26.00 or $57.00 for a group of sixteen people!

There is still a plan in the works to build a 100 site, RV oriented campground just outside the park near Almo. Originally the plan was to close all the currently used sites when the new campground was built, but that idea thankfully has been shelved. Still, the new RV park will severely stress the area simply by accommodating over twice the number of users as the City currently receives. Let park officials know how you feel about this.

LOCAL AMENITIES

Almo - 6.5 miles east of City of Rocks (Bath Rock). Tracy's General Store is still the place for groceries, aspirin, chalk, ice cream and **showers** all at fair prices. They have a pay phone, gas and the friendliest service this side of Nattimuk. These folks have been great friends to climbers over the years, so return the favor and spend tons of money there! The new store in town, the Almo Creek Outpost, is the closest place to buy beer.

Oakley - 18 miles. The road to Oakley is mostly dirt, but it's generally in good shape except after a rain, when the clay surface gets impassably slippery. This sleepy town has a good grocery store, a bar, a burger place and gas and even a town pool. Emergency auto repair is available. Of interest in cold and rainy weather is the **Warm Springs**, a commercial hot springs with indoor and outdoor pools. The springs are about six miles from town and are open Mon., Wed., Fri., and Saturdays from 1:00 to 8:00 pm.

Burley - 38 miles If it's mainstream commercial culture you crave, then this is the place. Burley is another 20 miles past Oakley and takes close to an hour by car from the City. Pinetree Sports carries climbing gear and can be found on the right (2165 Overland Ave.) soon after entering town. Showers can be had at the highway KOA or the truck stop by the interstate.

EMERGENCIES

If your party has a climbing or auto accident, first call **911**. If you don't have a cell phone it's probably best to go to Park Headquarters in Almo and let them take over. If the injury requires non-emergency medical care, you can go directly to the hospital at 2303 Park Avenue in Burley.
Emergencies 911
City of Rocks Headquarters (208) 824-5519
Cassia County Sheriff 678-2251

RATINGS

Difficulty ratings are an imperfect guide to what one can expect from a route. Routes protected with nuts and cams are a completely different experience from sport routes with closely spaced bolts. The element of danger on both trad and sport routes is an un-ratable factor, and the line between the exciting and the dangerous is in the mind of the climber. Beware, there are a lot of "exciting" routes at the City, both with and without bolts.

All the routes in this guide are fifth class, meaning a rope is recommended. In many instances the "five" prefix has been dropped, so 5.8 would be simply 8, and 5.11c becomes just 11c. Climbs with particularly poor protection are often marked with an "R" after the grade. "X" rated routes have little or no protection. Star, or quality ratings are pretty arbitrary, so feel free to make up your own list.

CLIMBING HISTORY

The early history of climbing at the City is shrouded in mystery. We do know that Utah climbers first visited the City as early as the 1950's, later forming the legendary Stienfell Club, with notable members Greg Lowe, Kent Christianson, Brad Roghar and others. The Steinfell crew bagged many fine crack lines in their day, but no one bothered to make a record of their approximately 300 routes.

Greg Lowe, probably the most talented climber in the group, was climbing at an amazing standard for the time. His 1968 ascent of *Crack of Doom* (11c) was perhaps the first 5.11 in the U.S. and certainly one of the City's most beautiful routes. Greg's other futuristic achievements include *Vice Grips* (11d), on the Building Blocks, the *Lowe Route* (11R) on the lost arrow and *Infinite* (11x), all done with relatively primitive foot ware and homemade protection.

By the late 70s The Stienfell club became less active, replaced by increasingly regular visits from climbers from around the region, especially Boise, Pocatello, Sun Valley, Jackson Hole and the Salt Lake City area. Still, not many people took climbing seriously back then, and a "crowded" weekend meant spotting another climber on a route somewhere.

As the popularity of the City slowly grew in the early 80's, climbers from the different areas began to get to know each other and keep tabs on what new stuff was going on. In 1982 Todd Skinner gave the area a shot in the arm by establishing two impressive routes, *Skinner's Roof* and *Electric Avenue*, both 11d/ 12a. Then, in 1983, Tony Yaniro moved into the area and quickly made news by climbing nasties like *Odyssey* 12a, *Rapture of the Deep* 13b and *The Boogieman* 14a. The latter may possibly still rank as the hardest crack climb in the world.

In '85, I printed a primitive guidebook and and wrote several magazine articles, which fed the City's growing reputation as a hot spot. The sport of climbing was very much in transition, with new wave "traditional" routes being more about mental control and bad protection than pushing physical limits. Naturally, many climbers were getting tired of the high risk, and craved the freedom of climbing without the fear of death.

In 1987, Darius Azin and Tedd Thompson first made use of a power drill at City of Rocks, on the aptly named *Power Tools* (12b).

Before long, energetic climbers like Jay Goodwin, Bill Boyle, Jeff Rhodes, Chris Barnes, Rex Hong, Mike Fischer, Dan Sperlock, Kevin Pogue, myself and others had drills, and "sport" routes were being established daily. In 1989 alone, a whopping 250 new routes were established. In just a few years, the City of Rocks had gone from an obscure rumor to an international destination.

For history's sake, it may be appropriate to acknowledge those who put out the effort and money to establish the routes that have made the City what it is. The following is a list (in alphabetical order) of the major route openers with approximate number of first ascents:

Tom Addison (17+), Pokey Amory (15+), Chris and Aimee Barnes (35+), Dave Bingham (100+), Bill Boyle (55+), Stan Caldwell (30 +), Reid Dowdle (15+), Jay Goodwin (30+), Mike and Dave Hatchett (10+), Rex Hong (15+), Greg Lowe (100+?), Kevin Pogue (10+), Brad Schilling (20+), Dan Sperlock (65+), Tedd Thompson (30+), Tony Yaniro (25 +).

In November 1990, the City of Rocks was designated a National Reserve and shortly thereafter a bolting ban was enforced. Many already felt that the City was "climbed out" anyway, but the ban clearly signaled the end of an era. The Pocatello gang went on to develop Massacre Rocks Idaho, SLC climbers had American Fork and Vegas, while Boise and Sun Valley climbers branched out to the infamous Leslie Gulch and a variety of basalt and limestone areas.

Ten years later The City is rarely in the news. Today's scene may lack the camaraderie and high energy of the late 80's, but the City is still one of the most beautiful places on earth to climb. New routes now require a permit and stainless steel hardware, but few permit applications have been rejected. Check with park headquarters for complete new route requirements. The potential for new climbs has exploded with new access, and new trails make it a cinch to get to the far corners of the Reserve. The City's history is still in the making.

WEATHER - GEOGRAPHY

The City of Rocks is located on the southeast slope of Idaho's Albion Range, an area known locally as the South Hills. The Range consists of a group of large rounded ridges which culminate in the glacially carved summits of 10,339 foot Cache Peak in the south, and 9,265 foot Mt. Harrison in the north. Cache Peak and its lower shoulder Graham Peak can be easily seen from the City. This small range juts up from the Snake River Plain like an island, catching the wind and weather that races in from the west. This explains why the City can be so damn windy, especially in the spring.

The summit of Cache Peak is accessible by trail from the Oakley / Elba road. A paved road climbs to the top of Mt. Harrison via the Pomerelle Ski Area access. Lake Cleaveland, located off this road, is a small alpine jewel and a nice summer getaway.

Most of the climbing areas at the City fall between 6,000 and 7,000 feet in elevation. Summer is often hot, but climbable in the shade. Luckily, most of the climbs are on east or west faces. In winter, the area receives severe weather and snow accumulations up to several feet. Generally the climbing season runs from April to November, sometimes earlier or later depending on the year.

GEOLOGY

Geologically, the City is part of the roughly forty square mile Almo Pluton, a dome of granitic rock or batholith which formed and cooled deep within the earth's crust. About twenty five million years ago, this "soft" granite intruded into the much older, metamorphosed gneiss of the Green River Complex. This older rock is of Pre-Cambrian origin, and is some of the oldest exposed rock in the continental United States. In the high areas surrounding the City you can also see the edges of the quartzite cap rock, which was uplifted by the granite intrusion. This unique "Oakley Stone" is imported all over the U.S. for flagstone and is prized for its tendency to split into thin sheets.

Over those last 25 million years, cracks and weaknesses in the granite intrusion eroded, leaving strings of granite islands - the rock formations we see today. Water passing back a forth in the outer layers of the rock has deposited an iron oxide layer on the surface of many rock faces.

This hard brown patina is what forms the solid edges, plates and "chickenheads" that climbers love. The bases of the rocks tend to erode faster than the patina coated rock above, causing the mushroom shape of some rocks and the common hard starts of climbing routes.

The rock quality at the City varies considerably, from a climber's standpoint. In general, the rock on the dryer west faces tends to be the best quality, often with a thick coat of lovely brown patina. The east faces are usually lower angled, and support more lichen and plants.

PLANTS AND ANIMALS

The environment of the City of Rocks is as unique as it is rugged.The big differences in elevation, wind exposure, moisture and soil type has produced a wide variety of plants and animal habitats. The extremes in climate promote an incredibly diverse species of plants (from desert to sub-alpine biomes) for this small area. In the lower elevations, sagebrush, juniper and piñon pine are the dominant plant species, while in the middle elevations these give way to stands of mountain mahogany and aspen, with alder and serviceberry growing along the creek bottoms. The higher elevations above 7,500 feet, are covered with groves of douglas fir, limber pine, lodgepole pine and windswept, grassy meadows.

The single-leaf piñon pine, which is prized for its tasty nuts, is common throughout the southwest, and reaches its northern growing range at the City of Rocks. A federally assigned "Research Natural Area" has been designated for the upper east side of the North Fork of Circle Creek, although no measures have actually been taken to preserve plant or animal habitat. Sadly, much of the natural ecosystem at City of Rocks has been severely altered by decades of cattle grazing.

Wildlife is fairly abundant in the area, but the relatively small pockets of vegetation types cannot meet the needs of large animal populations. Nonetheless, several species are common including mule deer, coyote, badger, porcupine, ground squirrels, bull snakes and lizards. The crags are habitat for birds of prey including turkey vultures, red tailed hawks, golden eagles and several types of owls and falcons. Less common animals include mountain lion, bobcat and peregrine falcon.

REGIONAL CLIMBING

In the last several years route development has exploded in obscure crags around the country. Idaho is no exception. The following is a very brief introduction to some of the new Idaho climbing areas, described from east to west. Some are day trips from the City, others are destination spots. Look for my new guide to these areas in the near future. Have fun exploring !

Heise & Paramount are on the north side of the Snake River about 20 miles east of Idaho Falls off route 26, en route to Jackson Hole. Heise is a small volcanic plug lovingly referred to as "Chuck's Choss Pile". There are a dozen routes from 5.10 to crimpy 5.13. Paramount is a more moderate crag on the hillside a mile or so upstream. Follow signs to the Heise Hot Springs. The crag is less than a mile past the springs on the left.
Pocatello has scads of short basalt rimrock crags with good quality rock. Ross Park, on the south end of the City, is the site of the annual Pocatello Pump contest and has a bunch of fun topropes and short leads. There is some good bouldering in the area as well. For more information, check in at Scott's Ski and Sports in town.

Massacre Rocks The good news is that Massacre is probably the largest and best collection of basalt climbs in the U.S.. Massacre has over **600 bolted sport climbs** on excellent basalt, spread out in a sandy, sheltered basin above the Snake River. The "back" areas are closest to the driving approach and have routes between thirty and eighty feet long, many equipped with quick-lowering top anchors. Closer to the river, the "Main Wall" is eighty to a hundred and forty feet high, in a pretty setting overlooking the river. Climbing can be done nearly all year if you pick the preferred exposure.

The bad news is getting there. The original approach was by crossing the Snake river in a canoe, kayak or whatever. This is still the best way to reach the "main wall", but obviously not many folks travel with canoes. The other option is to drive through American Falls, crossing the river at the dam, and following a not obvious route along the north side of the Snake River, finishing on marginal 2 wheel drive roads. Recently a landowner has closed the road, necessitating an even more involved backcountry drive with several fence crossings. For a full listing of Massacre Rocks routes and access check out www.isu/outdoor/massguid.htm

Howe - Box Canyon A new area featuring long (400 foot) bolted routes on good quality (but sharp) limestone. This unique high desert area is located at the toe of the Lemhi Mountain Range. Box Canyon currently has about 35 mostly moderate routes, and offers multi - pitch exposure with closely spaced bolt protection and anchors. The long routes require two 60 meter ropes and at least 18 quickdraws. There are also several spots for sport length routes, mostly moderate slabs in the 5.7 to 5.10c range. The "narrows" has half a dozen routes on superb, (but sharp) rock in the 5.10 to 5.12b range. Box Canyon is located eight miles northeast of the tiny town of Howe, off highway 33, about an hour northwest of Idaho Falls. You can camp in the canyon, but there are few flat spots and no water. Look for my up-coming guide "Idaho Climbs" for more information.

Pass Creek Pass Creek road bisects the Lost River Range a few miles south of the town of McKay. Pass Creek is a beautiful forested canyon with big, mostly crumbling limestone walls. There are, however, a few good routes and potential for more on solid patches of rock in the canyon. Existing routes are in the 5.9 to 5.12c range. Hidden Mouth Cave is an interesting spot to check out, also with some potential for new routes.

Bear Gulch Bear Gulch is accessed from Pass Creek about a half mile beyond the narrows to the left. This excellent quality crag was bolted ground-up style by Johnny Woodward and friends from SLC. Sadly, many of the 35 of so routes have sparse protection and fall into the sandbag category. If being scared is your idea of a good time, check it out.

Dierke's Lake / Shoshone Falls Five miles east of Twin Falls, Idaho is Shoshone Falls Park. Dierke's Lake is just upstream of the falls and is a popular summer swimming hangout for Twin Falls folks. Dierke's has great bouldering on chocolate brown basalt blocks, and a collection of wild (and a few not-so-wild) sport climbs. The "Alcove" is a nasty looking overhanging wall with very steep routes in the 10a to 12c range. If you like overhanging climbs with big holds, you will have fun here.

The bouldering at Dierke's is best in fall, winter and spring. The alcove gets hot in summer, so it's best to wait until the crag gets in the shade in the early afternoon. Dierke's is about a ninety minute drive from the City. It's a great retreat from the City on bad weather days.

Conner Columns Just north of the Conner Creek store, on the road toward Albion, is Conner Creek Summit. Look for the columnar basalt on the hillside east of the road. Take a right past a metal gate and up the steep dirt road, parking at the point closest to the cliff. This high quality cliff is only 30 to 70 feet high, but has numerous difficult crack problems. The routes may be led or top-roped. As of spring 2000, the only guide to the area is Mark Weber's "Idaho Basalt". The crag is about 30 minutes from the Cityof Rocks.

The Lava Caves Twenty miles north of the town of Shoshone are two lava tube "caves" that offer near horizontal sport climbing on huge holds. Routes range from 25 foot, four bolt crankers (11a to 13a) to seventy foot pump fests (10c to 13b) protected with beefy half inch bolts. There are seven or so routes in the shorter "little cave" and nine in the bigger "snake pit" cave. The caves are a two hour drive from the City of Rock, 40 miles south of Sun Valley. To find the Snake pit, turn right on the Burmah road one half mile south of the "Shoshone Ice Caves" entrance. Go a half mile then turn left on a dirt road. Park across from the fourth telephone pole. Walk due west (back toward the highway) through sage and lava for a couple hundred yards or so (5 minutes) until you see the fallen lava tube and cave wall.

For the little cave, turn right at the ice caves curio shop and drive about a hundred yards to an indistinct pullout on the right. Walk south through lava crust for a couple minutes to the collapsed tube /arch.

The Sawtooths A very pretty range, the Sawtooths offer some of the best alpine rock climbing anywhere. The prime attractions are multi-pitch crack routes on top secret crags like the Elephant's Perch, Finger of Fate and the Warbonnet cirque. The Sawtooths are about four hours north of the City of Rocks, and are a prime desti-nation for adventure seekers. Check the Elephant's Perch shop in Ketchum for info and topo's.

Swan Falls bouldering About an hour south of Boise is the famous "Birds of Prey" area. Nearby Swan Falls has a large area of basalt boulders with hundreds of problems. The area is kind of spread out, and having a bike along is nice. Hot in summer.

Boise Boise has two local areas worth checking out: Table Rock and the Black Cliffs. **Table Rock** sits above Boise and offers good bouldering, top-ropes and short leads on cool and unusual sandstone. Take Broadway to Reserve, then follow signs to Table Rock. **The Black Cliffs** are just east of town on highway 21 towards Lucky Peak Dam. There are more than 250 routes on the mostly southwest facing walls, making this a three season area, excluding summer. The climbs usually follow columnar features, with both sport and crack routes. See Sandy Epeldi's "Boise Climbs" for the full beta.

Leslie Gulch, Oregon This infamous spot is the home of Tony Yaniro's route building laboratory, a burly array of hard pocket routes skillfully carved out of a blank stone canvas. Yuk? If the concept disgusts you, as it does some people, pass on this one. But if you want to test yourself on some of the most spectacular climbs in the universe, a visit to Leslie Gulch is required. To find Leslie, take the sugar plant exit off interstate 84 at Nampa, then highway 55 south to Marsing. From Marsing go south on 95 for about 20 miles (over the big hills) to a right turn on McBride Creek Road. Drive dirt for another 25 miles to Leslie Gulch. Look for the amazing "flower petal" feature, "The Asylum" and park. The main crag, "The Einstein" is up the side gulch to the left. It's about a ninety minute drive to Leslie from Boise, or five hours from the City of Rocks.

Riggins Riggins is a long way from the City of Rocks and I've included it purely FYI. About two and a half hours north of Boise, the Riggins crags offer good limestone sport climbing. The main cave is one of the most amazing hard crags anywhere. With notoriously stiff grades, the routes start at 11d with most being in the solid 13 range. Above the main cave is another, more moderate crag with excellent rock. Check Boise climbing shops for driving directions.

Hells Canyon Limestone West of Cambridge on route 71, the
road dead-ends at Hells Canyon Dam. Ten miles this side of the
dam is an area of excellent quality limestone slabs, around Allison
and Eckles Creek. There are at least fifty mostly moderate (5.7 -
5.11) bolted routes just a short walk above the road. Good camping
is available nearby. Due to the low elevation of 1,600 feet, this is a
good cool weather destination, but it's stifling hot in summer.

NOTES

BIKING / HIKING / RUNNING

The building and improvement of over ten miles of trails at the City has been a major asset for bikers as well as climbers, runners and hikers. Now you have the option of embarking on longer, off-the-beaten-path tours or shorter loops on maintained trails. The longer loops typically involve travel on the main dirt road through the City and old two-track ranch roads. In most cases the back roads have become practically single track for lack of vehicle use.

The newly revamped trails that access Flaming Rock, Transformer, Bumblie Wall and the Lost Arrow are designated foot trails, and are closed to bikes. The new North Fork Trail, which starts by the Upper Breadloaves water pump, is also closed to bikes due to its fairly steep grades. Bike use on any of these trails could result in serious erosion problems.The following are descriptions of some of the great loops at the City.

The North Fork Trail - 6.5 miles (run/ hike) This newly built trail is my all time favorite trail anywhere. The awe inspiring views of the Circle Creek Valley are stunning. The trail begins across from the Upper Breadloaves water pump and climbs northeast along the western edge of the Circle Creek drainage. After a mile or so of climbing, the trail drops into the head of the North Fork and connects to the old road by Stripe Rock. Keep a sharp eye out for the spot where the Stripe Rock trail connects with the old road, it's easy to miss. From here you can cut back towards the Lost Arrow and join the South Creek trail (transformer area) either by taking the Boxtop trail or the more direct Lost Arrow / Bumblie Wall trail.

From the Transformer / Bumblie Wall area you have the choice of continuing up South Creek to the Parking Lot Rock area or climbing past Flaming Rock to the trailhead at campsite #39. From Parking lot rock, the new trail passes the Animal Cracker formation and junctions with the start of the trail just east of Shingle Butte.

South Creek/ Flaming Rock Loop - 2 miles (run / hike) This loop begins at the Boxtop Trailhead, by site #19 and Practice Rock. Follow the old road / trail that drops down to South Creek from the knoll just east of Practice Rock. Cross the creek and look for the trail heading back left (west) up South Creek, back to Flaming Rock.

South Creek / Parking Lot Rock Loop - 3.5 miles (run / hike) You can start this loop at either the Boxtop trailhead (site # 19) or the Flaming Rock trailhead (site # 39). After descending from the camping areas to the aspen groves along South Creek, follow the new trail that leads up the creek beyond the Slabbage Patch. This trail meanders up to the east side of Parking Lot Rock after passing near the Drilling Fields, and the Redtail area on Rabbit Rock. From Parking Lot Rock, the scenic route is to loop back around the west side of Creekside Crag and come out at Bath Rock, then take the road (duh) back to the trailhead (or camp site) where you started.

Logger Springs Road - (Bike) This is the grueling grade that leaves the main road a half mile west (toward Oakley) of the Upper Breadloaves. The maintained dirt road climbs past Finger Rock, and continues climbing to over 8,500 feet, or about 1,900 vertical from the junction with the City road. A good loop is to grind to the saddle about 3/4 mile past Finger Rock, then follow an old road that drops east into **Indian Grove**, a pretty hanging valley with an amazing view of the City. The trail/ road from the saddle is a super downhill of about 1000 vertical back to the Upper Breadloaves by the outhouse. Other options include an out-and-back up to Indian Grove from your campsite, going up to Indian Grove and down Logger Springs Road, or poaching the North Fork Trail to Stripe Rock and back to camp.

Trail Creek / Twin Sisters Loop - 8 miles (Bike) A moderate loop of two-track and dirt roads. Take the old two-track road that climbs west from Elephant Rock past the Nematode and Private Idaho. From Private Idaho the road drops down Trail Creek past the Obvious Wall for about a mile to a point where you need to take a lesser track up to the left. Look for the rock formations that mark the saddle between Trail creek and the Sisters drainage. It's less than a quarter mile up to this saddle. From the saddle, follow the sandy road along the west side of the Twin Sisters ridge and connect with the main road at the Sisters. Finish the ride with 3 miles of dirt road back to Elephant Rock. Note: this ride crosses private land. Always leave gates as you find them, open or closed.

Emigrant Canyon Loop - 8 miles (Bike) This is a fairly mellow ride on primitive two-track with historic ambiance. Start at the Twin Sisters, going south on the main road. After one downhill mile, take the Emigrant Canyon road to the left. This road passes between two hills then hits the flats of the upper Raft River Valley after about 2 1/2 miles. Turn left on another two-track that skirts the east side of the hill, and keep left when you reach yet another two-track that heads back to the Sisters Road. If you keep left you can't get lost.

City of Rocks Circumnavigation 14 miles (Bike) This ride takes you high above the City on the Indian Grove two-track to about 7,300 feet and then down Graham Creek to a low point of 5,500 feet just west of Almo. Any way you ride it, there is a solid climb of 1,800 vertical, mostly on the main dirt road. Take the main road from your campsite to the Emery Canyon Saddle at the Upper Breadloaves. The road to Indian Grove heads north, just across from the out-house. There is an old sign painted "no trespassing" at the gate, so be super low profile if you decide to trespass. Follow this two-track past a rock formation on the left, looking for a old road that cuts right (east) and down. Descend this old road down Graham Creek toward the Castle Rocks and the town of Almo. You will cross several fences before reaching the maintained dirt roads west of Almo. Be sure and close the fence gates. Once on the road, stay right for about a mile to where this road intersects the main City road. From here it's a beefy grind back to where you started the ride.

Use the overview map on page 6 for reference or the USGS Almo quad, which is available at park headquarters in Almo.

RECOMMENDED ROUTES

5.3 -5.6 Many of these easier routes are exciting and rewarding summit scrambles to the top of rock formations. These routes tend to have minimal protection, and require more mental control and route finding skills than technical ability.

Lookout Ridge*   Not often roped, A very worthy summit. p.48
Cowboy Route*   Bath Rock. 2 pitches of easy fun. Bring slings for horn pro. p.42
Easy Way Up* - Bath Rock. Easy. p.48
Dykes on Harleys* -Decadent Wall p.16
Watersports* - Decadent Wall p.16
Easy Movements*   A nice slab in the Sisters area. p.104
Window Rock** -Summit Route. A very cool summit with arch. p.29
Easy Corner** Provo Wall. Fun! p.19
Morning Glory*   A bold venture to the top. Hard start. p.35
Pure Pleasure** - Window Rock. Crowded. p.29
Good Times** - Window Rock. Crowded. p.29
Juniper Jam* - Window Rock. p.29
Rabbit Rock Summit   Route finding, exposed. p.33
Hesitation Blues* - Rabbit NE p.32
The Suns Edge* - Clamshell. 2 pitches. p.79
First Lead* - Practice Rock. p.61
Norma's Book**   A classic. p.26
North Sister South Face** - 2 pitches. Fantastic summit. p.99

5.7
Hough's Crack* - Super Hits p.18
Intruding Dike** - Super Hits p.18
Adolescent Homo** - Decadent Wall. p.16
Triple Roofs* - Provo Wall. p.19
Fledgling* - Owl Rock. Crack. p.20
No Curb Service* - Parking Lot Rock. p.26
Swiss Cheese** - Anteater. Scary. p.36
Miki's Six* - Bumblie Wall.Runout slab. p.59
Rain Dance** - Flaming Rock. Well traveled slab. p.57
Wheat Thin** - Elephant Rock. One of the top five. p.66
Classic route** - Lost arrow. A must do. p.80
Cruel Shoes** -Stripe rock. 3 pitch bolted slab. p.88

Dike of Gastonia* Stripe Rock. p.88
Practice Rock Cracks** p.61
Open Y-D* - Heartbreaker Rock. p.78
North Sister - Guides Route*. 3-4 pitches. p.99
Theater of Shadows** -Jackson's Thumb. 4 pitch bolted route. p.93

5.8

Fred Rasmussen* - Upper Breadloaves. Crack classic. p.14
Catwalk** - Upper Breadloaves. p.14
Carol's Crack** Decadent Wall. A nice thin crack. p.16
Twist and Crawl** Super Hits. face / arete. p.18
Humble's Tumble* Provo Wall p.19
Batwings*** - Parking Lot Rock. An excellent long pitch. p.26
Snack Break Direct** - Owl Rock. Stout for the grade. p.20
Snakes and Ladders** - King on the Throne. p.21
Indian Summer* - Window Rock. Thin pro. p.29
Delay of Game*** - Parking Lot Rock. Bolted face. Crowded. p.26
Morning Glory Chimney* - Morning Glory Spire. p.35
Skyline*** - Morning Glory Spire. Super Classic. p.35
Smuckers Jam* - Creekside. Wide crack. p.43
Too Much Fun*** - Bumblie Wall. Bolted face. Crowded. p.59
Rye Crisp*** - Elephant Rock. Bold laybacking. p.66
Strawberry Slam* - Elephant Rock. p.64
Driving At Night* - Odyssey. p. 76
Corridor Crack** - The Boxtop. p.77
Crack-A-Go-Go* - Stripe Rock. p.88
Modelo* - Great Wall. 2 pitch trad route. p.90

5.9

Lost Pioneers** - Upper Breadlaoves. Thin, leaning crack. p.14
Aspen Leaf** - Upper Breadlaoves. Cool stemming. p.15
Streachmarks** - Upper Breadlaoves. Classic short corner. p.15
Devine Decadence* - Decadent Wall. p.16
A Finer Niner** - Provo Wall. Bolted face. p.19
Snack Break** - Owl rock. p.20
Z - Cracks** - King on the Throne. Crack in corner. p. 21
Pocket Rocket* - Window Rock. One move to easy slab. p.29

Funky Bolt* - Parking Lot Rock. A nice crack. p.27
Suburban Sprawl** - Parking Lot Rock. Bold but really fun.p.26
Scream Cheese*** - Anteater. Bolted Face. p. 36
Dire Straights** - Creekside. Tricky pro at start. p.42
Mystery Bolter** - Transformer. Bolted slab. p.58
Just Say No** - Elephant Rock. p.66
Boxtop Traverse** -Boxtop. Wild. p.77
Boxtop Summit* - Boxtop. p.77
Vertical Turtle* - No Start Wall. Offwidth / Chimney. p.81
Banana Peel* - Banana Crag. p.92
Inner Circle** - Inner Circle Rock. A hard version of "Swiss Cheese". p.49
Barf Crack** - Sisters. A crack classic. 106
South Shoulder* Sisters. Cool old fashioned route. p. 101
Old West Face** - South Sister. 4 pitches, Route finding. p.101
Yellow Wall*** - Sisters. A really neat route. 110

5.10a
Decadent "L" ** - Decadent Wall. Bolts to anchors. p.16
Double Vision** - Super Hits. p.18
Bloody Fingers*** - Super Hits. Best 10a crack in the City? p.18
Tennish Anyone?** -Provo Wall. Bolted face. p.19
Double Cracks** - King on the Throne. p.21
Stan's Roof* - King on the Throne. p.21
Animal Cracker** - Animal Cracker Dome. Great old fashioned route. p.30
Batwings Direct* - Parking Lot Rock. p.26
Tow-Away Zone** - Parking Lot Rock. A great route. p.27
Beauty and the Beast* - Parking Lot Rock. p.27
Thin Slice** - Parking Lot Rock. Very nice crack / stem. p.27
Book of Dissent* - Morning Glory Spire. great chimney / crack.p.35
Holding out for a Hero** - Anteater. kind of bold. p.36
Coffee and Cornflakes** - Bath rock. p.54
Tribal Boundaries*** - Flaming Rock. p.56
Short Circuit* - Transformer. 10a unless you're short. p.58
New York is not the City* - Bumblie Wall. Popular.Bolts. p.59
Deez Guys** - Slabbage Patch. Steep face with bolts. p.60
I Can't Believe It** - Slabbage Patch. Easy for the grade. p.60
The Pygmies got Stoned* - Elephant Rock. Bolts. p.64
Just Say Go*- Elephant Rock. Bolts. p.66
Acid Rain* - Building Blocks. Bolts. p.84

5.10d

Beyond good and Evil** Shangra-La. p.11
Impotence* Decadent Wall. Bolts. Fun. p.16
Self Abuse** Lower Decadent Wall. Bolts/gear. Excellent. p.17
Box Lunch** Lower Decadent Wall. Bolts/gear. Well worthy. p.17
Rhodan* Owl rock. Hard moves, small pro. Exciting. p.20
Brown Flake** Morning Glory Spire. p.35
Harvest** Window Rock. A thin crack testpeice. p.28
A-Rester* Rabbit Rock. Crack. p.33
Flyboy* Anteater. Bolts and pins. Fun and out of the way. p.36
Terrebone Jacks** The Office. Bolts and gear. p.38
Lost Soles* Lost World. Bolts / friction. p.41
Loner with a Boner** Obvious Wall. Bolts. p.47
Prepare for Soaring Seagulls* Elephant Rock. Mixed bolts and gear. p.64
Pocatello Punk* Elephant Rock. Mixed bolts and gear. Contrived but fun. p.66
Big Pig** No Start Wall. Long, fun traversing pitch. p.81

5.11a

Make it Hurt More* Go West p.10
Urban Renewal* Upper Breadloaves. Wild. p.14
Interceptor** Upper Breadloaves. Classic crack. p.10
Flesh for Fantasy* Decadent Wall. Bolts. p.16
Just Hold Still** Lower Decadent. Bolts p17
Riding on an Incline* Provo Wall. p.19
Psycho Driller* Provo Wall. p.19
The Awakening** King on the Throne. Gear and bolt. p.21
Terror of tiny town*** Buzzard Perch. One of the best. p.31
Redtail*** Rabbit Rock. Long and popular. Bolts. p.34
Sudden Pleasure** Rabbit Rock. Bolts. p.34
Cairo*** Parking Lot Rock. Short but sweet arete. p.27
Pigs on a Wing* Drilling Fields. Steep bolted face. p.40
Science Friction** Lost World. A well bolted slab. p.41
Siesta** Morning Glory Spire. Cool moves on perfect rock. p.35
Scar Tissue*** The Office. a must do gear route. p.38
Pogemahone** Lower Creekside Tower. Bolts on a steep face. p.44
Prey for Me** Bath Rock. Bolted arete / face. p.53
White Hueco's* Bath Rock. p.46
Loch Ness Monster** Bath rock. Bolts. p.54

White Line Fever** Private Idaho. Great rock, bolts. p.47
Chomping At the Bit** Transformer. Bolts and gear. p.58
Bumblie takes a Tumblie** Bumblie Wall. Bolted face. p.59
Forcash and Riches* Lost Arrow. Short bolted face. p.80
Master Mechanic* Boxtop. Bolted arete. p.77
Technoweenie** Building Blocks. p.84
Scrapps** Building Blocks. p.84
Straight Edge*** North Sister. Bolts and gear. Mega. p.99
Safecracker** North Sister. Bolts. p.99
Safer than Sex** North Sister. Bolts and gear. p.99
Milky Way* South Sister. Bolts. p.100
Fly like an Eagle* Eagle Rock. Bolts and gear. p.107

5.11b
Bad Manners* Upper Breadloaves. Way Wild. p14
Provo** Provo Wall. Cool moves w/ bolts. p.19
Bovine Guidance*** Nematode. Bolts and gear.
Crack of Doom*** Morning Glory. The best line in the City. p.35
Dance to the Music** Rabbit Rock. Technical face.Bolts. p.33
Hyperspuds** Rabbit Rock. Bolts and gear. Excellent. p.34
The Drilling Fields** Bolts on steep rock. p.40
Such a Slabbage* Slabbage Patch. Bolts and gear. p.60
Crotchbound* Private Idaho. Bolts. p.47
Firewater** Flaming Rock. Sweet patina.. p.56
Spot** Electric Ave. Bolts. p.62
Ball and Chain** Electric Ave. Steep! p.62
Same Place, Different Girlfriend* Electric Ave. Bolts. p.62
Some Assembly Required* Checkered Demon. p.63
Routine Expedition** Boxtop. Bolts. p.77
Surfing the Orgasmic Wave** Heartbreaker. Bolts, gear. p.78

5.11c
She's the Bosch*** Window Rock. long bolted face. p.28
Strategic Defense*** Morning Glory Spire. Gear and bolts. p.35
Spud Meets Hammerhead* Parking Lot rock. Bolted slab. p.27
Rio* Rabbit Rock. Bolts. p.33
Moderne Zieten** Creekside. Excellent moves. p.43
Bumble Pie* Bumblie Wall. Bolts. p.59

Unknown Bumblie* Bumblie Wall. Bolts. p.59
Fido** Electric Ave. Bolts. p.62
Fluid Dynamics** Nematode. Bolts. p.68
Blast' f' me* Bath Rock. Bolts. p.53
Static Cling** North Sister. A very cool route. p.99
West with the Night* Secret Tom's. Bolts. p.113

5.11d
Testosterone Test** Decadent Wall. Bolts and gear. p.16
Bubo Bulge* Owl Rock. p.20
City Fathers* Rabbit Rock. Bolts. p.32
Seasonal Employment** Rabbit Rock. Bolts and gear. p.34
Midlife Crisis** Rabbit Rock. Bolts and gear. Wild. p.33
Dressed to Kill**Rabbit Rock. Bolts. p.33
Rabbit Wrestling* Rabbit Rock. p.34
Body English* The Office. Scary. Gear and bolts. p.38
Snake Charmer* Creekside. Long bolt route. p43
Tarantula* Bath Rock. Fun. p.54
No Self Control* Hummingbird corridor. Bolts. p.48
Last Request* The Dungeon. Powerful. Bolts. p.62
Technicon*** Building Blocks. p.84
Terms of Endurement* North Sister. Bolts. p.99
Bulldike* Bulldog Wall. Bolts. p.103

5.12a
East Provo* Provo Wall. p.19
Fat Lip** Buzzard Perch. Wild. Bolts. p.31
Bombs Over Tripoli** Parking Lot Rock. Bolts. p.27
Gemini** Bath Rock. Clean moves. p.54
Nairobi** Creekside. Sustained and technical.Bolts. p.42
Calamari** Bath Rock. Steep. Bolts. p.53
Smoke Signal** Flaming Rock. Athletic & fun. Bolts. p.56
Electric Avenue*** Gear. Classic line. p.62
Young Frankenstein** Electric Ave. Roof. Bolts. p.62
Udder Delight** Crystal Cow. Short but sweet. p.48
Odyssey** A trick move to a awesome crack. p.76
Sizzler* No-Start Wall. p.81
Power Pig** No-Start Wall. Very nice. p.81
Body Buster** Lost Arrow. Sustained. Bolts. p.80
Cracka-jawea* North Sister. Long pitch with bolts. p.99
Skinner's Roof** Sisters Area. A off-hands crack. p.109

5.12b

5.12c

5.12d

5.13a

5.13b

5.13c

INDEX

W

Y

Z